Writing to Save a Life

John Edgar Wideman's books include *American Histories, Philadelphia Fire, Brothers and Keepers, Fatheralong, Hoop Roots* and *Sent for You Yesterday*. He is a MacArthur Fellow and has won the PEN/Faulkner Award twice and has been a finalist for the National Book Critics Circle Award and National Book Award. He divides his time between New York and France.

ALSO BY JOHN EDGAR WIDEMAN

Fanon: A Novel

Briefs: Stories

God's Gym: Stories

The Island: Martinique

Hoop Roots: Basketball, Race, and Love

Two Cities: A Novel

The Cattle Killing: A Novel

Fatheralong: A Meditation on Fathers and Sons, Race and Society

All Stories Are True

The Stories of John Edgar Wideman

Philadelphia Fire: A Novel

Fever: Stories

Reuben: A Novel

Brothers and Keepers: A Memoir

Sent for You Yesterday: A Novel

Damballah: Stories

Hiding Place: A Novel

The Lynchers: A Novel

Hurry Home: A Novel

A Glance Away: A Novel

American Histories: Stories

Writing to Save a Life

JOHN EDGAR
WIDEMAN

CANONGATE

Published in Great Britain in 2018 by Canongate Books Ltd,
14 High Street, Edinburgh EH1 1TE

canongate.co.uk

1

First published in 2016 in the United States by Scribner,
an imprint of Simon & Schuster

In this work, which is an amalgam of research, memoir, and imagination, I have changed the names of some of the people and places that appear and in a few instances have created composite individuals

British Library Cataloguing-in-Publication Data
A catalogue record for this book is available on
request from the British Library

ISBN 978 1 78689 372 7

Printed and bound in Great Britain by Clays Ltd, St Ives plc.

MIX
Paper from
responsible sources
FSC® C018072

Dedicated to prisoners

Looking through steel bars at a guard, the prisoner said:
I am sad to see how unhappy you are in your cage

all stories are true . . .

CHINUA ACHEBE, *THINGS FALL APART*

CONTENTS

I

LOUIS TILL

One of my grandfathers, John French, my mother's father, taller, skin a shade lighter than many of the Italian immigrants he worked beside plastering and hanging wallpaper, used to ride me on his shoulders through the streets of our colored community Homewood in Pittsburgh, Pennsylvania. I loved to sit up there. Safe. King of the world. Entranced by my grandfather's tales about the neighborhood, by his long silences, his humming, his rhymes and songs. His broad shoulders a sanctuary I would count on, even when my father disappeared periodically from various homes shared with my mother and me.

I have never forgotten how peaceful the world looked from up there. How one day while I rode on my grandfather's shoulders, my hands, knees, careful not to tip his wide-brimmed, brown hat, we passed Clement, a smallish man who swept out Henderson's Barbershop. But back then, at this precise moment in the Homewood streets, I knew nothing about Clement, except I could see he limped, dragging along one worrisome foot in an oversize boot, and see he had a big face ugly enough to seem scary, even from my perch, a face with distorted features I did know would loom in my nightmares for years afterward.

John French called out the name *Clement* and the man returned the greeting with a slowly forming but finally huge grin, openmouthed, few teeth, a lingering gaze that fixed upon us, then inside us, then wandered far, far past us. A look telling me that everything familiar to me could instantly be unsettled and dissolve.

In 1955, about nine years after that encounter on the Homewood streets, I was fourteen years old, and a photo of dead Emmett Till's mutilated face entered my life with the same sudden, indelible truth as Clement.

Just in case you don't recall, I'll remind you that in 1955, Emmett Till, also age fourteen, boarded a train in Chicago to visit family in Mississippi. A few weeks later a train brought his dead body back to Chicago. Emmett Louis Till had been murdered because he was a colored boy and had allegedly wolf-whistled a white lady.

Over half a century later, I'm still dealing wih the faces of Clement and Till. To provide background for a fiction I intended to write about Emmett Till, I saved excerpts from newspaper coverage of the trial of Till's muderers.

Over sixty newspapers on hand in 1955 for the Sumner, Mississippi, trial. Thirty photographers popping flashbulbs, seventy reporters pecking away at truth on their typewriters. I was a bit surprised by how much national and international attention the trial had attracted. Not surprised to learn public interest had rapidly evaporated. Today Emmett Till is generally viewed as a civil rights martyr, but the shabby trial that exonerated his killers, and the crucial role played by Till's father in the trial have largely disappeared from the public's imagination. Silenced, the Till trial serves as an unacknowledged, abiding precedent. Again and again in courtrooms across America, killers are released as if colored lives they have snatched away do not matter.

> . . . the day opened hot and humid, the heat rising to an almost unbearable 95 degrees. (*Chicago Defender*)
>
> . . . townspeople of Sumner have never seen anything like it here—the crowds, the out-of-state newsmen and the excitement of a big trial—not even on Saturdays or when merchants conduct a drawing to give away an automobile . . . Citizens estimated as many as a thousand outsiders came, more than on the biggest trade days . . . a porter kept busy passing a pitcher of ice water to trial officials. Downstairs, a cold drink stand had its biggest day in history. (*Memphis Commercial Appeal*)
>
> Twenty-two seats were provided inside the rail for white newsmen where they could easily hear the proceedings . . . Negro press . . . limited to four seats directly behind the rail where the public is seated. (*Chicago Defender*)
>
> A lily-white jury overwhelmingly constituted of farmers, all of whom have sworn bare-faced against all their traditions that it will not affect their verdict that the accused are white men like themselves and the victim a Negro boy from Chicago. (*New York Post*)
>
> . . . the judge laid down the rules . . . He stated that smoking would be allowed and suggested that the men take their coats off for comfort. (*Chicago Defender*)

. . . Defendants made a dramatic entrance with their attractive wives and children at 10:25 a.m., setting off a buzz of interest and lightning-like flashes from the combined action of thirty cameramen . . . Mrs. Carolyn Bryant, a 21-year-old brunette who is expected to be a key witness, was dressed in a simple dark gray dress with a high neckline. Bryant held his two sons, Lamar Bryant, 1, and Roy Bryant, 2, and Milam clutched his boys, Harvey Milam, 2, and Bill Milam, 4 . . . Milam said he has been a good friend of the Negroes he has known. He said five years ago he plunged into the Tallahatchie River, from which the body of Emmett Till was pulled, and saved the life of a drowning seven-year-old Negro girl. (*Memphis Commercial Appeal*)

Once, Bill Milam picked up a toy pistol . . . fired an imaginary shot at Roy Bryant Jr. . . . clambered over the rail and stomped down the aisle making little boy noises . . . ran his hand along courtroom railing pickets, apparently deriving great satisfaction from the machine-gun click-clack he produced. (*Memphis Commercial Appeal*)

Moses Wright pointed a knobby finger at J. W. Milam today and said, "There he is"—identifying him as one man who abducted the sharecropper's nephew in the early morning hours of August 28. Then the 64-year-old farmer pointed out 24-year-old Roy Bryant, Milam's half-brother, as the second man who roused the Wright family from bed at 2:00 a.m. and took Emmett Louis Till away . . . "I got up and opened the door . . . Mr. Milam was standing at the door with a pistol in his right hand and a flashlight in the other," Wright declared. (*Greenwood Commonwealth*)

Q: What did Milam say when you let him in . . .
A: Mr. Milam said he wanted the boy who done the talking at Money . . . [Mr. Milam] told me if it was not the right boy he would bring him back and put him in bed . . .
Q: When was the next time you saw Emmett?
A: He was in a boat where they had taken him out of the river.
Q: Was he living or dead?
A: He was dead.
Q: Could you tell whose body it was?
A: It was Emmett Till.
Q: Did you notice a deputy sheriff taking the ring off his finger?
A: Yes. (*Jackson State Times*)

Chester Miller, Greenwood undertaker, took the stand for a second time and described Till's body: "The whole top of the head was crushed in. A piece of the skull fell out in the boat," he said, ". . . I saw a hole in his skull about one inch above the right ear." . . . Sheriff H. C. Strider of Tallahatchie County has said a bullet caused the hole above Till's ear. (*Greenwood Commonwealth*)

Sheriff Strider has said the body may not be that of Till. "The whole thing looks like a deal made by the NAACP." (*Jackson Daily News*)

The judge allowed the defense to record Mrs. Bryant's testimony with the jury out of the room.

Q: Who was in the store with you?
A: I was alone . . . At about eight o'clock a Negro man came in the store and went to the candy case. I walked up to the candy counter and asked what he wanted. I gave him the merchandise and held out my hand for the money.
Q: Did he give you the money?
A: No.
Q: What did he do?
A: He caught my hand in a strong grip and said, "How about a date, baby?"
Q: What did you do then?
A: I turned around and started to the back of the store, but he caught me at the cash register . . . He put both hands at my waist . . . He said, "What's the matter, baby, can't take it? . . . You needn't be afraid."
Q: Did he use words that you don't use?
A: Yes.
Q: It was unprintable, wasn't it?
A: Yes. He said that and added "with white women before" . . . Another Negro came in and dragged him out of the store by his arm. (*Jackson State Times*)

A young Negro mother returned today to her native Mississippi to fight to avenge the life of her fourteen-year-old son . . . Mrs. Mamie Bradley Till, 33, is a demure woman whose attractiveness was set off by a small black hat with a veil folded back, a black dress with a white collar. In the more than 99 degree heat of the courtroom, she fanned herself with a black silk fan with a red design . . . In a quiet voice she answered the questions of the newsmen . . . (*Daily Worker*)

Q: Where did you first see the body?
A: I saw it at the A. A. Rainier funeral home in a casket . . . I positively identified the body I saw in the casket as my son . . . I looked at his face carefully. I looked at him all over thoroughly. I was able to see that it was my son's body without a shadow of a doubt.
Q: His father, Louis, was killed overseas in the armed forces, was he not?
A: Yes, sir.
Q: Were his father's personal effects sent to you after his death.
A: Yes, sir.
Q: Was there a ring in those personal effects.
A: Yes, sir.
Q: Did you give your son the ring that was returned?
A: Yes, but his hand was too small to wear it at the time. However, since he was twelve years old, he has worn the ring on occasions, using scotch tape or a string to help it from coming off. When he left Chicago, he was looking for some cuff-links in his jewelry box and found the ring and put it on his finger to show me that it fit and he didn't have to wear tape anymore.
Q: And you say definitively that he left Chicago with the ring in his possession?
A: Yes, sir. (*Jackson State Times*)

Milam shook off his kids yesterday afternoon and stood up all by himself at adjournment and asked, "Where are our goddamned guards? We've got to get out of here." (*New York Post*)

Up rose Sidney Carlton for the defense to point out the holes in the state's case . . . He said of course Mamie Bradley, a mother, believes what she wants to believe. "The undisputed scientific facts are against her." Then J. W. Kellum rose for the second defense summary . . . "I want you to tell me where under God's shining sun is the land of the free and home of the brave if you don't turn these boys loose . . . your forefathers will turn over in their graves." (*New York Post*)

"What is your verdict," inquired the court. "Not guilty," said Mr. Shaw in a firm voice. The two defendants were all smiles as they received congratulations in the courtroom . . . lit up cigars after the verdict was announced. (*Memphis Commercial Appeal*)

Mississippi Jungle Law Frees Slayers of Child . . .
An all-white jury of sharecroppers demonstrated here Friday that the constitutional guarantees of "Life, Liberty, and the Pursuit of Happiness" do not apply to Negro citizens of the state. (*Cleveland Call and Post*)

Fair Trial Was Credit to Mississippi . . .
. . . Mississippi people rose to the occasion and proved to the world that this is a place where justice in the courts is given to all races, religions, classes. (Greenwood, *Mississippi Morning Star*)

In my notebook, the newspaper excerpts end with the words of Chester Himes, a colored novelist who chose not to reside in his segregated country and probably sent his letter to the *Post* from Paris, France:

> The real horror comes when your dead brain must face the fact that we as a nation don't want it to stop . . . So let us take the burden of all this guilt from these two pitiful crackers. They are but the guns we hired. (*New York Post*)

As I read more about the trial, I discovered that the jury had deliberated less than an hour—*sorry it took so long, folks . . . we stopped for a little lunch*—before it delivered a not guilty verdict. For an American government waging a propaganda war to convince the world of Democracy's moral superiority over Communism, intense criticism of the verdict abroad and at home was an unacceptable embarassment. Federal officials pressured the state of Mississippi to convict Milam and Bryant of some crime. Since abundant sworn testimony recorded in the Sumner trial had established the fact that Milam and Bryant had forcibly abducted Emmett Till, the new charge would be kidnapping. Justice Department lawyers were confident both men would be found guilty.

Except, two weeks before a Mississippi grand jury was scheduled to convene and decide whether or not Milam and Bryant should be tried for kidnapping, Emmett Till's father, Louis Till, was conjured like an evil black rabbit from an evil white hat. Information from Louis Till's confidential army service file was leaked to the press: Emmett Till's father, Mamie Till's husband, Louis Till, was not the brave soldier portrayed in Northern newspapers during the Sumner trial who had sacrificed his life in defense of his country. Private Louis Till's file revealed he had been hanged July 2, 1945, by the U.S. army for committing rape and murder in Italy.

With this fact about Emmett Till's father in hand, the Mississippi grand jury declined to indict Milam and Bryant for kidnapping. Mrs. Mamie Till, her lawyers, advisers and supporters watched in dismay as news of her husband's execution erased the possibility that killers of her fourteen-year-old son Emmett would be punished for any crime, whatsoever.

Revisiting trial testimony did not help me produce the Emmett Till fiction I wanted to write, but I did learn that his father's ring was on Emmett's finger when he was pulled dead out of the Tallahatchie River. The ring a reminder that Emmett Till, like me, possessed a father. A Till father I had never really considered. A colored father summoned from the dead to absolve white men who had tortured and shot his son.

While I gathered facts for an Emmett Till story never written, a second encounter with Louis Till occurred. In the mail I received an unsolicited galley of *The Interpreter*, a biography of the French novelist Louis Guilloux, author of *OK, Joe!*, a fictionalized account of his job as interpreter at trials of American GIs accused of capital crimes against French citizens during World War II. *The Interpreter*'s author, Alice Kaplan, used Guilloux's experiences to examine the systematically unequal treatment of colored soldiers in United States military courts during World War II.

I found myself quite moved by Kaplan's description of her pilgrimage to the grave of Private James Hendricks, hanged for murder by the U.S. Army in 1945, a colored soldier at whose trial Louis Guilloux had worked. Kaplan's book took me 120 kilometers east of Paris, to *a part of the countryside where the fiercest battles of World War I were fought—a gentle landscape of rivers, woods, and farmland, interrupted by an occasional modest village.* I arrived with her at a *massive World War I cemetery, with its iron gates and stone entry columns.* Stood finally in a clearing enclosed by laurel bushes and pine trees reached by exiting the back door of the cemetery administrator's quarters. The clearing contained Plot E, the officially designated "dishonorable" final resting place of ninety-six American servicemen executed by the U.S. military during World War II.

Situated across the road from Plots A–D, where 6,012 honorable American dead from World War I are buried in the main cemetery of Oise-Aisne, Plot E is quiet, secluded, seldom visited, meticulously groomed. A place unbearably quiet, I imagine, as I read Kaplan's depiction of Plot E in *The Interpreter* and surveyed with her eyes an expanse of green lawn dotted with small white squares she discovers are flat stones embedded in the crew-cut grass. Four rows of stones, twenty-four stones per row, the rows about five feet apart, every white square engraved with a gray number, she writes.

I accompany her, moving slowly up and down the slight slope, between the rows, because when you stand still, Plot E's quiet is too enveloping, too heavy, too sad. I need to animate my limbs, stop holding my breath in this almost forgotten site where ninety-six white squares mark the remains of men, eighty-three of them colored men. What color are the eighty-three colored men now. What color are the thirteen other men beneath their gray numbers. I think of numbers I wore on basketball and football jerseys.

Numbers on license plates. Numbers tattooed on forearms. My phone number, social security number.

On page 173 in chapter 27, the final chapter of Kaplan's book, she narrates in a footnote how she reaches number 73, the corner grave in row four that *belongs* to Louis Till. His *story has such tragic historical resonance,* she writes, then informs the reader of Private Louis Till's execution by the army in 1945 for crimes of murder and rape in Italy, and that ten years later in 1955, Till's fourteen-year-old son Emmett was *beaten, shot, and thrown in a river in Mississippi for whistling at a white woman.*

With research of Emmett Till's murder fresh in my mind, I had wanted to inform page 173, inform Alice Kaplan the wolf whistle was only one of many stories, a myth as much as fact, though I didn't speak to her then, in the shared quiet of Plot E whose silence I feared breaking even as I also understood I could not break it. Instead I raise my eyes from the page, my gaze from the photograph of a numbered white square of stone, and disappear, a ghost in the machine of a book, machine of my body. I do not speak to Alice Kaplan in Plot E. It's not the time or place to discuss the wolf whistle's problematic status. Not the time now to expand this anecdote about finding Louis Till in Kaplan's book nor to talk about my own trip, years later, to the French cemetery. This is just a brief version of encountering Louis Till. Anyway, I believe the truth is more like he found me than I found him.

Dear Professor Kaplan,

In your account of a visit to Plot E of the Oise-Aisne American Cemetery and Memorial on Sunday afternoon in January 2004, you relate that the look-alike white grave-markers were engraved with gray numbers and not names.

How could you identify the person buried beneath a particular stone. More specifically, how did you know Louis Till was under stone 73. Had you obtained a directory, a guidebook, some official document matching names with numbers. If you possess such a source, where did you discover it. Would you be willing to share it. Does it contain facts about the dead other than names and numbers. Did you have in hand a map of Plot E so that you anticipated finding Louis Till's grave at the corner of row four. Were you touched equally by the Till grave and the grave, number thirteen, of Private James Hendricks, the colored soldier whose trial you feature in your book about French novelist Monsieur Louis Guilloux, the interpreter at James Hendricks's court-martial. Were you struck, Professor Kaplan, by the coincidence that both Mr. Guilloux and Mr. Till bear the given name *Louis* or by the resemblance between *Guilloux* and *guillotine.* Did you feel on the Sunday afternoon you explored Plot E that the life of each one of us no matter how tightly we clutch it, is an unanchored thread that does not guide us out of the labyrinth. I thank you in advance for any information you're able to offer about these matters. Your book *The Interpreter* led me to Plot E of the Oise-Aisne American Cemetery and Memorial, and in a very real sense I have been wandering since in a limbo inhabited by shades of men buried there.

Several years after that letter—never sent—I was shaving and the TV news talking in another room announced a black father declared guilty of protecting his son. A carful of mad white boys rolls up to the black man's suburban Long Island driveway and they demand he surrender his son to them because the son they say insulted the sister of one of the boys. A sexual, racial trespass, thus unforgivable, thus the son must pay. But the daddy, an old-time emigrant from the deep south, got a long memory, got him a little pistola cached away for just such emergencies. *No. No. Never again.* Get thee gone, ye whited sepulchers, he goes or says other words to provoke a predictable riposte such as, *Nigger, you better move your scrawny old black nigger ass out of the way, boy,* an exchange I imagine escalating rapidly to nastier imprecations and threatening gestures terminated abruptly by a single gunshot. One white boy down, bleeding on the black man's driveway. The other boys in his crew rush him to the hospital, but it's too late. He dies on the way, and this morning the breaking news: a judge has pronounced the black father guilty.

Familiar script. *Offended white males go after black boy accused of molesting white female.* Same ole, same ole Mississippi Till story repeating itself, but with the roles, the scenario sort of scrambled—north not south, day not night, black guy not white guy the one with a pistol in his hand, white accuser dies, accused black boy survives, and the court in this New York case declares black shooter guilty, not like Mississippi law declared the white shooter of Emmett Till innocent. This latest version of the script altered but not enough to obscure its resemblance to the original. Then the point would be lost, wouldn't it. Just enough alike and different to appear as if festering ugliness between blacks and whites changes. Though it really doesn't change, except maybe for the worse. This is what I heard from the TV in the other room as I shaved.

And getting even worse day by day it seems when I pay attention—one more colored victim declared guilty without a trial falls, fallen, falling dead, here, there, everywhere . . .

* * *

This text will not become the Emmett Till fiction I believed I was working on. All the words that follow are my yearning to make some sense out of the American darkness that disconnects colored fathers from sons, a darkness in which sons and fathers lose track of one another.

When I call the National Archives in Washington, D.C., the person, a specialist in military service records a friend suggested and whose extension I ask for, is unavailable. The phone of an alternative clerk, to whom I'm referred by a friendly human operator whose voice identifies him as alive and colored, picks up after three rings. A recorded message offers another extension that plunges me into a cycling menu of instructions, the product of Starquest Answering Service that's either unintelligible by design or designed to make me pay for my sins—sins of age, of poor hearing and unnimble fingers, of unfamiliarity with the latest maneuvers necessary to wield control over recorded voices offering choices. Each set of options is so lengthy I forget them if I listen to the entire list. Or choose prematurely, always incorrectly, if I don't listen to the bitter end. I feel like poor Ulysses roped to the mast, teased by a chorus of sirens or baffled, like Ralph Ellison's invisible man by voices whose job is to keep me running. Voices that chirp, chatter, lecture, and sometimes, I'm sure, chortle at my efforts to steer through them and obtain information about Louis Till.

Turns out the backup person I seek is not available either, I learn later from the friendly colored operator. The alternate person's mother died suddenly and he's away burying her in

Alabama. The toll mounts. Casualties jinxed perhaps by mere association with the grim subjects of my inquiry: kidnap, rape, murder, execution by hanging.

After weeks of calling and reaching no one, I complain again to the live voice. He offers yet a third number and bingo, persistence seems about to pay off. The original archivist who'd been reported gravely ill is either back at his desk or at a virtual desk in heaven where he's able to receive calls. His voice is music to my ears even though it's recorded music. He/it promises to return missed calls promptly, and sure enough my call's returned. A recorded voice offers a number, recited twice to make sure I get it. I'm elated. Hang up immediately, punch in the twice-repeated number, and alas, find myself adrift in Starquest again.

Leghorn, Italy, a.k.a. Livorno, the site of Louis Till's court-martial, say documents arriving at last, at last, after I put my request to the government in writing. The Louis Till file mailed to me also states that the executions of Till and his codefendant, Fred A. McMurray, occurred in Aversa, Italy, near Naples. I welcomed such facts though they only led to more questions. According to the death certificates of Privates Till and McMurray, the men were hanged the same day—July 2, 1945. Little else about the executions in Aversa appears in the copious file. Did Till and McMurray drop simultaneously, each through his own trapdoor, at the conclusion of the same . . . 3 . . . 2 . . . 1 countdown. Who counted. One countdown or two. One double scaffold or two scaffolds, separate and equal. Were the condemned offered a last chance to speak. Did either avail himself of the opportunity. Who witnessed the ceremony. Did the U.S. Army invite townsfolk and town officials, as was occasionally the practice at executions of American soldiers in occupied France. In Brittany, for example, the public execution site of a colored G.I. is remembered in the Breton language as *park an hini du*, black man field.

Was a real doctor or army-trained medic assigned to listen for the absent pulses of dead Till and McMurray. Sunshine or rain that day. Did the condemned meet their fate resolutely or falter. What thoughts were they thinking on the gallows steps. How many steps. Were the steps wooden. Portable. Were photos taken of the living prisoners, dead prisoners. What archive holds them if they still exist. Much later I would find in a book, *The Fifth Field*, a few photos claiming to document the hangings of Till and McMurray. Are the photos authentic. Is Louis Till's face truly one of the faces in the blurry snapshots.

A copy of a Battle Casualty Report (July 20, 1945) appears on an early page of the Till file and registers Louis Till's death. The words "in Italy" are typed crookedly into the *Place of casualty box*. An asterisk occupies the box where *Type of casualty* is supposed to be recorded. At the bottom of this page, just beyond the Casualty Report's edge, a footnote, indexed by the asterisk above, contains two phrases, "judicial asphyxiation" and "sol died in a non-battle status due to his own misconduct." Mrs. Till asserted on numerous occasions that only the second phrase was included in the telegram of July 13, 1945, sent to inform her of her husband's death.

Given many such willful or unavoidable or contested or careless or premeditated aporias in the official account, how could the most diligent researcher hope to accurately reconstruct a double hanging in Aversa, Italy, over a half century after it happened.

Where there's life, there's hope, my mom used to say, even though my father, if he happened to be around, would always interject: *And for every tree, there's a rope,* a rejoinder that would have irritated Mom even more if she had known (and probably she did) it was the punch line of a joke making fun of a southern darky *ha-ha-ha* obsessed with copping him a taste of white pussy *ha-ha* before he dies.

Where there's life, there's hope

Did Louis Till ever cop a taste of leghorn. Some historians contend the city of Leghorn is named for chickens its earliest settlers found in residence when they arrived to erect a fortified town in the middle ages. Others argue leghorn chickens—a small, hardy domestic fowl noted for prolific egg production—are named for the city where they were originally bred. Though the city of Leghorn, near Genoa in northwestern Italy on the Ligurian Sea, played a prominent role in his short (twenty-three years) life, it's probably safe to conjecture Louis Till could not have cared less whether chickens or city bore the name *leghorn* first. But did he ever sample the local bird. Louis Till probably *knew* chicken in the sense Charlie Parker (a.k.a. *Bird* for love of them) knew chicken, but whatever Louis Till thought about leghorns or the city of Leghorn is lost in the silence that confronted me when I sought his voice in documents from the file.

Malcolm (a.k.a. Malcolm X) who shares a family name *Little* with the famously paranoid bird Chicken Little, was not literally present at Louis Till's trial and execution, but Malcolm informed the world in no uncertain terms why proverbial chickens on their way home to roost in America would have paused in Leghorn/Livorno and clucked disapproval of the kangaroo court-martial conviction and hanging of colored privates Louis Till and Fred A. McMurray. Louis Till, my father and most other veterans of World War II, colored and not, are gone now and humankind is no closer to solving problems created by the conundrum of race than we are to figuring out whether leghorn chickens or their eggs came first. I attempt to smile and nod reassuringly as I promise Louis Till, Mamie Till, my father, brothers, sister, mother, Emmett Till, Malcolm, Martin, Mandela et cetera, that some of us are absolutely not satisfied by the prospect of remaining forever in the dark. Darkness as deep and sinister as the dark in which many colored soldiers, executed like Till and McMurray and James Hendricks, lie buried.

All stories are true. As far as I've been able to glean, Louis Till possessed no knowledge of that particular Igbo proverb, nor a general familiarity with the customs and folklore of the Igbo, a West African ethnic group whose homeland is southeastern Nigeria (a.k.a. Biafra). Even if Till had been a prolific reader, he would not have come across *all stories are true* in Chinua Achebe's *Things Fall Apart*, where I first read the proverb. Achebe's novel, set in a traditional Igbo village at the beginning of the twentieth century, was not published until 1958, thirteen years after Louis Till's death. Yet it seems that Till was privy to the wisdom of *all stories are true.* In the only direct quote attributed to him by army officers in the entire Till file, Louis Till articulates a very Igbo understanding of the predicament in which he found himself.

According to report #41 (Criminal Investigation Division/

Rome Allied Army Command, United States Army—7 August, 1944) filed by CID/RAAC agents I. H. Rousseau and J. J. Herlihy and included in the Till documents I received, Louis Till didn't open up to any extent when Herlihy, posing as a fellow prisoner, confined himself (10 July 1944) in the brig with Till to gain information about the crimes—assault, rape, murder—of June 27–28 in Civitavecchia, Italy. Another attempt to secure a statement from Till on 23 July 1944, the report continues, also met with negative results. Till remained adamantly silent, offering no information about the crimes being investigated nor providing an alibi to establish his whereabouts on the night of June 27. A stubborn silence that must have puzzled and frustrated his army interrogators since all the other accused colored soldiers were busy accusing one another. Breaking his silence once in response to the agents' repeated demands for a statement, Louis Till allegedly said to Rousseau, "There's no use in me telling you one lie and then getting up in court and telling another one," a remark that clearly conveys to me and should have conveyed to Rousseau, Till's Igbo sophistication, his resignation, his Old World, ironic sense of humor about truth's status in a universe where all truths are equal until power chooses one truth to serve its needs.

If not in Achebe's book, where did Louis Till learn the proverb's wisdom. Louis Till was probably not good at reading. Not a devourer of paperback westerns like my father. Different as they were, both men were the same deep brown color, I believe, and both boxed. Both men, like traditional Igbo wrestlers, honed their bodies to school their minds. Both were good enough with their fists to try amateur boxing. My father in Pittsburgh, Till in Chicago, according to Mamie Till's autobiography.

I see Louis Till in a gym—bobbing, weaving, feinting, throwing punches. Hear him training as I turn pages of the Till file. Heavy bag—*whomp, whomp.* Speed bag—*blippidity—blip—blippidity—blip—blip.* Sugar Ray fast hands flick out quick, quicker. Till up on his toes, leans in, dips back, circling—*blip—blip—blip—blip-pidity*—the bag can't get away quick enough. Till tags it. Stings it. Snaps his punches. Sweat flicks off his dark shoulders. Then *hop-hop-hop-hop* he's skipping rope—arc of jump rope cuts slices of air, tongue-shaped, round-shouldered tombstone slices inscribed a thousand perfect times. They hiss over him, behind him, portals of frozen air which frame a snapshot of Louis Till each time the rope whips by. Only inches to spare. Top of Till's head sliced clean off if he doesn't duck, step, lean, hip-hop through the whizzing rope.

Been there, done a little boxing myself. Recall how a jump rope dies a split-second *whap* as each arc strikes the floor. *Whap-whap-whap* under Till's feet. In canvas shoes, quick hop after little quick hop seems like the boy don't hardly touch the ground—he's flying—the spinning rope whaps the gym's wood floor—*whap—whap*—like slaps in the face. Wooden handles of jump rope gripped in taped fists, Louis Till carves the shape—tomb-stone, tongue—one last time. Ducks under, ducks through. He's winded. Sweat drips. He freezes. Still as stone a couple counts, then attacks the speed bag again, relentless until he's finished and lets the bag wobble to a stop. Walks away wet head to toes. Skinny calves, thick thighs, thick torso, a pigeon-toed walk like they say the fastest runners walk. Till heavyset, but light on his feet, sneaky quick, a silent Indian kind of walk and isn't that why she's so quiet, Mamie Till so still, holding her breath, waiting for Louis to return.

Mamie Till is difficult to pick out in the apartment's deepest shadowed corner where she's slumped. She doesn't want Louis Till to see her before she sees him. Quiet as a mouse so he won't hear her before she hears him and launches her attack or counterattack, she tells herself, hiding from her husband in the darkness with a butcher knife and pot of boiled water with a lid to stay hot, scald his sorry ass, his mean soul. He hurt her first. Louis Till hurt her bad and she's still hurting an hour later, back pushed against the wall, knees pulled up, chin resting on her swollen breasts, breasts resting on her big belly, the poor little child inside her made to go through all this ugly shit, too. Not even born yet but here's her baby, his baby in the dark crying and hurting like she is, her poor baby inside her moaning like she'd moan out loud if the noise wouldn't give away her hiding place. Mamie Till is all drawn up inside herself, quiet-quiet, hard-soft ball of herself, round and crowded up with the scared baby inside, she waits. Mamie righteous, fierce, because to save her child she must save herself. She must counterattack and drive Louis Till out the door.

Mamie Till told an interviewer Emmett almost missed his train to Mississippi. She said they had to hurry to get to the Twelfth Street Station on time. I believe I've seen that station, that it's in the documentary I watched, *Say Amen, Somebody,* about the origins of gospel music, featuring Willie Mae Ford, legendary Chicago singer. I replay a scene in which the middle-aged daughter and son of Willie Mae Ford drive down a ramp into a train station's underground parking lot. Stroll with them up to street level. Peer with them into a window near an unused entrance to the station. Our faces press close to the glass. With tissues from her purse, the daughter scrubs at a thick coat of grime. *Boy, oh boy. Look at that.* The camera meanwhile previews the station's dark interior—an old-fashioned passenger coach abandoned on the tracks where it was uncoupled last, giant cylindrical metal containers stacked against a wall, unrecognizable debris scattered everywhere, gathering dust and rust in the gloom. *Coming down here and seeing this decay, based on what it used to be, my, my, puts it all in one package,* the man says to his sister, both of them standing inside the station now, eyes panning like the camera. *My, my,* the man sighs, close to tears. He recalls for his sister the station's better days, a busy hub of activity when their mother was a star on the gospel music circuit, *funny how every time those redcaps be knocking each other out the way to pick up Mama's luggage.* Not about tips. *No, no. You know Daddy. Daddy didn't believe in tips. Huh-uh. A dime sometimes maybe, most they gon get, if they got that.*

Grainy clips earlier in the documentary had shown Willie Mae Ford, gospel queen in furs and feathered hats, departing or returning home to Chicago. Freedom trains full of colored emigrants from the south used to land many times a day in Chicago, trains whose sounds are embodied in the old, new music Willie Mae Ford sings, music baptized "gospel" by Reverend Thomas Dorsey, a.k.a. *Georgia Tom,* a blues troubadour in his younger days. Dorsey's gospel music too bluesy for some folks. Too much Bessie Smith, Mamie Smith, Ida Smith hip-shaking, home-breaking in it, explains *Say Amen, Somebody,* and not everybody ready to hear it inside their churches. *I remember when lots of them wouldn't have Mama to sing let alone preach,* the sister says to her brother.

The train station in the video could be the same one where September 2, 1955, Mamie Till, dead Louis Till's wife, dead Emmett Louis Till's mother, accompanied by her father, an uncle, cousins, an undertaker, two preachers, one named Louis Henry Ford (the father of Willie Mae Ford?) wait for the train from Mississippi bringing her murdered son back home to Chicago. Same train, the *City of New Orleans,* Emmett had boarded alive to leave Chicago less than two weeks before. A large crowd congregated at the station on September 2 to support Mrs. Till and witness the terrible truth of a story read in the papers, passed by word of mouth, concerning one of theirs, a fourteen-year-old Chicago black boy on a summer visit to relatives in Money, Mississippi, a boy beaten, shot, his mutilated body wired by the neck to a seventy-pound cotton gin fan and tossed into the Tallahatchie River to punish him, his cousin's story claims, for wolf-whistling a white woman.

The tape plays on and I listen for the Till train's entry into the station. Listening as I still listen some Sunday mornings for the scratchy music from my mother's cracked black plastic radio tuned to WAMO at the end of the dial. My fair-skinned mother humming along as she spray-starches and irons one of my brown-skinned father's white shirts for church. White shirts with collars and breasts ironed stiff, my father wears under his waiter's jacket six days a week downtown in a dining room in Kaufmann's department store in Pittsburgh, a restaurant that used to be barred by a gold rope across the entrance, by a hostess notoriously uncordial towards colored folk who dared to eat there. Louis Till must have owned a white shirt. My father's white shirt for church Sunday morning was more perfectly white and gleaming than the perfect ones worn to work every weekday and Saturday. My father's hardness and absence crackled in those white shirts he demanded be kept spotless, wrinkle-free. In a room rented after he left us for good, gospel plays on a radio while he removes a laundered white shirt from its cellophane wrapper. He turns his back to me to put it on. When he's facing me again, I watch his thick, dark fingers button the shirt, tremble to work gold-rimmed cuff links into tiny holes.

Even as a boy fourteen years old, Emmett Till's age when

Emmett Till was murdered, I understood my father hated those white shirts. Hated them and loved them, too. I also understood, boy or not, I was a large enough boy to get my ass out of bed and help my mother the night I heard a terrible crash in our living room. I knew my parents were fighting, but instead of rushing to save my mother, I lay petrified, pretending to sleep, afraid of a white shirt glowing in the darkness of the adjoining room. I held my breath, waited for my mother's footsteps to prove she was alive and had managed to pick herself up from the floor.

My father had been waiting for my mother. I knew this without spying on him. How could I sleep while my father sits out there waiting for my mother, waiting with the lights off in the other room, not a sound for hour after hour except music playing in my head and the snoring of my siblings. Rakhim in bed beside me was the worst. On good nights the other kids' restlessness and nasty noises were quieted by sounds of my mother busy in the kitchen, scrubbing dirty pots, rinsing, drying, stacking dishes. The rasp of a crooked cupboard door that never shuts first try. The last thing every evening she runs water for a cool drink then washes her cup and puts it away for coffee next morning. Same cup she uses all day so she doesn't *make extra work*. Plate, knife, fork and spoon set out for my father each night he's not home for dinner so he knows there's food in the fridge to warm up if he hasn't eaten on the job or smuggled home fancy leftovers from late night private parties he works. Last final thing, she switches off the kitchen light, and the yellow bar under our bedroom door dims.

Some nights I keep listening after my mother leaves the kitchen, crosses the living room, into the hall. Listen past the point she's probably asleep in the tiny room squeezed into a corner of a landing at the top of stairs that go down to the Lemingtons' apartment. My parents' room is a room far enough away to muffle their whispers, their preparations for sleep on those rare nights they go to bed together. Though certain nights, I think I hear the blue crackle of a white shirt as my father pulls it off, or hear my mother alone in their bedroom humming gospel like she hums when she's up very late waiting for my father to come home and he doesn't, and she hums herself to sleep curled on the couch. Always gone when I jump up first thing next morning to check.

No matter how long I listen, sooner or later my vigil fails. I drop off and lose her. Worst nights, lying awake beside my youngest brother Rakhim, I worry and worry that everything I love and hate will be gone in the morning and never return. I listen long after my mother finishes her last little things, turns off the kitchen light and the bright inch under the door is replaced by faint illumination leaking in from a lamp by the front door she always leaves on for my father. I wonder if my mother's sleeping or not in the bedroom, more closet than room, where she's supposed to be. Wonder if she's full of worries about my father. My siblings. Me.

The night of the terrible crash came right after three days and nights my father never made it home. Not home late as usual. Not home early or late. Not ever. No father for three days. No warnings in the morning from my mother to the younger kids, *Shhhh. Hush all that noise, youall. Shush and eat your cereal. You know your father's sleeping. You know you better not wake up your father.* No father's snores when I pass the bedroom landing on my way to school.

On the bad night my father returns early. Nine, ten o'clock. Very early for him, anyway, and he knocks softly then fumbles in his deep pockets for keys to let himself in. My mother's out. Very late for her. A rare night she's not home, and good boy me has performed his duties, bedded down the other kids at the exact hour, in the precise fashion, almost, my mother commanded. *Don't be mean to your little brothers and sister. Firm but nice with them. And don't you dare sit up waiting for me like you think you're my mother. Soon enough I'll be sitting up all night worrying because you think you're grown enough to run the streets till dawn,* she said. But I couldn't help staying awake.

Music's playing in my head, fast and slow, rhythms change, words change, Rakhim's wheezing snores mixed in, blues mixed with gospel, mixed with R & B, the Dells and Diablos, Drifters and Spaniels and Midnighters singing my songs on WAMO. Love music mixed with worry music mixed with dance music mixed with desire and fear of things I didn't know the names of yet. Worried maybe I never would. Worried it all might vanish.

No light brightens the crack below the door. My father snapped it off when he came in and discovered my mother not at home. After three days gone, I'd begun to believe he'd left for good, but then I hear his key in the lock and he's back home that night before my mother. Mother late. Father early. Strange turnabout. Me faking sleep. I wasn't spying on my father, but I could hear his breathing, heartbeats, pounding of his thoughts, his big hands gripping his knees. I could hear his stillness in the overstuffed armchair everybody called Daddy's Chair. His impatience and anger fill the silence with unthinkable acts, unspeakable words, hard and heavy as fists.

I pretended not to know why I was scared, though if I had tried, I could have said why. I was old enough to understand nearly everything. It was all in the music. In the talk in Henderson's Barbershop. *Woman who's a wife and mother got no damned business out in the street, don't care whatever goddamned sister you say you with, no goddamned business out in the street this goddamn time of night.* Did I hear those particular words that night or are they blues words, gospel words, barbershop words dreamed, heard before the fact or after the fact of my mother's body striking the floor, a sound that would have awakened me even if I'd been asleep as far away as the place old thunder and lightning, fire and brimstone Reverend Felder of Homewood AME Zion promised God would pitch bad black boys.

The singer's daughter tells her brother she overheard one of the church young folk ask: *Willie Mae Ford Smith. Who that?* Then *Say Amen, Somebody*'s camera retreats for a long shot to frame the once-upon-a-time gospel queen's children within the airplane hangar immensity of an empty steel shell with steel girders holding up a steel groined, vaulted ceiling, the section of a Chicago train station they reached by driving earlier in the video down a ramp at whose entrance light blazed in a checkerboard pattern from overhead grates, shafts of smoking brilliance pouring into the obscurity below, obscurity only slightly relieved here, inside the station, by illumination from begrimed panels in a ceiling miles away it seems from where the brother and sister stand now after they have parked underground, exited outdoors, then entered the station. They instinctively huddle closer together as they talk in whispers, as any two people or small group of persons likely would talk in a gloomy space that dwarfs them, dwarfs their voices whether they speak softly or shout. Big-boned, wide-hipped, large brown people whispering small things, simple, deep things, a call-and-response of reminiscence, holding on, letting go until there is no bottom, no sides, no ceiling to the station, no secrets, no down or up or come or go.

I pause the tape. Is it the Twelfth Street Station. What does it remember. Is a train station able to gaze at itself, revive the past, double it, a double as quiet as the face, the moving lips of my reflection within a mirror. Quiet as silences within the silences of Thelonious Monk's piano. During the Twelfth Street Station's heyday did people's dreams truly float above the platform upon which I picture myself waiting for an Illinois Central train to arrive or depart, a platform lined with cardboard suitcases, ancient steamer trunks, duffel bags, shopping bags, string-tied bundles and cartons, colored girls carrying everything they own in a warm package they cradle in their arms, all of that dreaming and waiting, waiting, every shadow and echo and breath of those lives dust and grit somebody brooms away each morning from the station's concrete floor.

I remember Chicago at night, a tapestry of winking, blinking lights out the windows of an elevated train, lights which are pinpricks in a black winding sheet draped over a snowbound city. And once in a taxi, approaching the city in daytime from O'Hare, I stared at the stark verticality of church steeples, minarets, smokestacks, waves of skyscrapers, a gray backdrop that recedes and draws nearer, both at once, skeletal towers trussed by power lines, sheaves of dirt poor dirty row after ramshackle row of houses, blocks of low-rise apartment buildings, public housing warrens twenty stories high, acres of demolished blocks, blocks and succeeding blocks of concrete, brick, stone-faced canyons the hawk rules in winter and no matter how much you bundle up or hoody-up humping through alleys, wind-tunnel streets, body slanted at a forty-five-degree angle like a character in a cartoon, your eyes tear, teeth chatter, no mama to wipe your snotty nose.

I also remember Chicago in a photo tucked in an old family album. Who had scribbled *Chicago* and people's names on the photo's yellowed backing. Faded, indecipherable names. Names of dressed-up folks maybe on their way to a splendid party. Chicago was a surprise in the Pittsburgh family album. Who are these strangers floating past, fancy people, handsome people in furs and expensive overcoats, my sturdy brown people light on their feet as ghosts. Do they live on another planet inhabiting the planet I inhabit. One scene, one photo, many universes dissolve, splash, one into the other always. I still possess Emmett Till's photo from September 1955 on a page torn out of *Jet* magazine that Aunt Geraldine saved and gave me thirty years later.

I was fourteen the first time I saw the photo in *Jet*. Emmett Till's age that summer they murdered him. Him colored, me colored. Him a boy, me too. Him so absolutely dead he's my death, too. Fuzzy replicas of the photo appeared in colored newspapers—*Pittsburgh Courier*, *Chicago Defender*, *Amsterdam News*—the image circulating, recycled decades later in *Eyes on the Prize*, a documentary history of the civil rights movement in which I saw the horrific picture of dead Emmett Till's face staring back from my TV screen and freeze-framed it. Courage mustered finally, half a century after the fact. I did not look away. Hoped if I stared hard maybe the photo would wither, wrinkle, flames curl its edges, consume it. No screams, no agony, no sputtering frying chicken crackle like you'd think you'd hear.

I push play and *Say Amen, Somebody* resumes. More quiet exchanges between brother and sister, their voices barely audible to one another above the stillness. Are they afraid words might disturb sleeping ghosts. Delay the Till train's slide into the station or its glide away. As if words could stop a train. Stop time. No. Not even words a brother and sister keep inside themselves, *will you bury me or will I bury you,* not even those unsayable words shouted out loud could waken their mother, stop the Till train.

Willie Mae Ford Smith's grown-up children under the steel arc of roof remember fine clothes, fine cars, taxis. Black limos rolling up to the curb. So much glitter and glamour. The brother recalls veteran redcaps as well as neophytes shaking their heads in wonder, *Who that. Where they going. Where they coming from. Boy oh boy.* Their mother, Willie Mae Ford, sang church music thick with blues, ready or not, like it or not, you get blues licked up in gospel. *Didn't want Mama when she young and just starting out, and before long they standing in line in bitter cold and snow paying good money to hear Mama and now the young folks see her in church every Sunday forgot her name.*

Later, leaving the station, one sibling frowns, the other grins in response. Whole lifetimes flicker on the TV screen compressed into a single glance they exchange. One expression scrubbed away instantaneously by the next, light to dark to light, too fast to follow, he's your brother, you're his sister, we've done that, been there, no need to go back, to linger or regret or hope. Here we are, here it is, this quiet moment in the station Samboing into every other moment and the black boy chases the tiger fast as the tiger chases him.

Mamie Till listens harder than anyone else for the Till train. Looks closer than anyone else at her dead son's body, *I looked at the ears, the forehead, the lips, the nose,* she wrote. She knows the train's due, perhaps in the station already, the same *City of*

Orleans that carried her live Emmett away two weeks ago, returns today with his corpse, enters the Twelfth Street Station, enters silence sealed under a high, arching ceiling. Silence of dark, swollen thunderclouds, quiet of a storm ready to burst.

ARGO

Nothing closer to truth than truth—but the truth is—not even truth is close to truth. So we create fiction. As a writer searching for Louis Till, I choose to assume certain prerogatives—*license* might be a more accurate word. I assume the risk of allowing my fiction to enter other people's true stories. And to be fair, I let other people's stories trespass the truth of mine.

I go with Mamie Till back home to Chicago. It's a week or two after the Mississippi murder trial and its ugly aftermath. No kidnapping charges filed against the two men who abducted and killed her son. *Why* Mamie Till is asking herself. Mrs. Till, dead Emmett's mother, dead Louis Till's wife, must be thinking that terror never ends. Terror is truth and truth is terror and it never ends, she thinks. Truth of that big stinking crate with a box inside with Emmett's dead body inside the box. Terror of the box closed, truth of the undertaker prying it open with hammer claws. Terror of not looking, truth of looking. She must bear both for Emmett, for love, for justice, a look inside the box she cannot dare until she prays hard and a voice whispers, *your heart will be encased in glass and no arrow can pierce it.* Truth of listening to herself say, *I want the world to see what they did to my baby.* Terror of standing beside Bo's open casket at the funeral while she sees in the eyes of mourners who file past the terror and truth of what they see. Terror of lost Emmett. Truth of how he returns. *There's my heart underneath that glass lid.* Terror of sleepless sleep, sleep, sleep, sleeping all day, never truly asleep. Truth of being wide awake forever, day and night. Terror and truth of nightmares sleepless sleep brings . . .

She talks to herself. After the ceaseless terror and truth and terror, she's still alive in her mother's apartment in Argo and must decide to live or die, and decide again the moment after this one. Yes or no again. Her eyes rest on a man who sits on a chair Albert carried in from the kitchen. This man, the half brother of her lover Albert, has the strange name, *Wealthy*, and she thinks maybe he might have been sent by God, to help her. She needs to believe, needs help. Too many nights alone, too much wandering and fumbling around here in these rooms alone day after day, bone tired, going crazy, if truth be told. No sleep, then more tired and nervous fumbling around here after Mama goes off to work in the morning. I'm all alone with my own self, she thinks, but keep bumping into Bo, my sweet Bo, everywhere and then it's not him I hear, I smell, I follow. I reach out to touch him, but Bo's gone, gone, and I drop down on the sofa or armchair, try to nap, to forget and can't. Wear myself out trying to make up some person who will tell me what to do next, tell me to stop holding my breath, tell me how to breathe again, tell me not to wait for the worst thing on earth to be over because it's never over, always more terror and truth and then more.

Mr. Wealthy looks like a nice man and I surely do need somebody nice, a nice somebody to say words I can't say to myself. Say breathe. Say the thing you must do next, Mamie Till, is this. The voice of a new somebody. Not you, Mama. Not nice Albert. Somebody I don't know who says words I need to hear. No face, no color, no man or woman I can imagine, though I think it should have to be a man because a woman's too much like me, she would try to make me feel better because she's a woman, a mother who understands bleeding inside for her child and moaning inside and watching how everything outside minute by minute pays you no mind, gets no better, gets worse and you're more scared every minute for your child but nothing you can do, just watch and hurt and bleed and try to tell yourself it's not as bad as it seems, everything going to be all right like the songs say, by and by, but that lie don't fly, you are just talking to your own dumb self, you need another person to tell you the truth. It could be a woman or a man who tells it to me but harder, Mama, to believe a woman and nobody, no man or woman or chicken with a talking mouth can bring back my child. My sweet Bo gone. They killed my baby.

They said Emmett bad, Mama, and say that's why he's dead. Bad like his bad daddy, *like father like son* they said and I need someone to talk to me, hold my hand. I need kind words doesn't matter who says them, and when this half brother or cousin or friend or whatever of my Albert, this Wealthy, his odd name, comes to the door, I ask myself is he the answer to a prayer I only halfway allowed myself to pray, prayed so softly under my breath, couldn't hear myself praying it was so quiet and so deep down inside me because I wasn't sure I wanted God to hear either, maybe just overhear, didn't want God to get the wrong idea that maybe I blame Him or always expect nice things from Him or like I know better than Him what's right or wrong for me or think I deserve His special attention when I don't because this whole wide world like you say Mama ain't nothing but a stool for Him to rest His feet on. Just bear the burdens the Good Lord give you to bear, girl, Mama says. He ain't never gon burden you with more'n you can handle, she says. And sure enough here comes this man Wealthy. He doesn't know me, never knew Louis, never met Bo. Here he is out the goodness of his heart in my mama's apartment in a polka dot tie and a nice gray suit he wears like he's in the army, all buttoned up, pressed and starched soldier sharp like Louis grins picture perfect clean in his army photo. This Mr. Wealthy not a strapping man like Louis or Albert. A smallish, tight fist kind of man, iron creases in his clothes and straight-backed as an arrow and proper the way he took a seat on the chair Albert carried in from the kitchen and Mr. Wealthy straightens his neat little self, tugs his silver tie, as if one too few polka dots showing. Tugs a pant leg straight after he crosses a short leg over his knee.

No ma'am. No thank you, ma'am. Nothing to drink for me, thank you, Mrs. Till, the first thing he says after he said, Pleased to meet you, ma'am, though I'm truly sorry we are meeting under these unhappy circumstances, Mrs. Till. Same words she heard from the lemon-colored undertaker, Mr. A. A. Rainier, who buried Emmett, undertaker smiling his sad, droop-mouth smile at people so he gets that check when they're grieving for somebody or somebody grieving for them. Mr. Rainier says pleased to meet you, Mr. and Mrs. So and So, sorry it's under these circumstances, fresh graveyard mud on the wingtips of his shoes, spit-shined like Mr. Wealthy's shoes, Mr. Wealthy with one narrow foot standing at attention in the air, the other foot patting Mama's living room rug after he crosses his little leg over his knee and begins to speak.

Don't you believe a word those dogs say, Mrs. Till. Excuse my language, please, ma'am. Albert told me many times what a fine young man you were raising. Albert very fond of your son, Emmett. You all have my deepest sympathy, Mrs. Till. You and your family and Albert, too. Wished I could do something to help and thought to myself it's not much but it's the least you can do, Wealthy, go on over there with Albert and tell Mrs. Till about the army. Army something I know, Mrs. Till. I'm a veteran. I know the army and I can tell you from experience. Army lies. Tell a person every kind of lie there is. Bad business they put in the newspaper about your late husband, best not believe a word of it.

Army and the government lie. Lie, lie, lie all the time. When the sneaky Japs bomb Pearl Harbor, plenty of us colored men in a hurry to join the army. We want to enlist because it's our country, too. Only country we got, and it's a man's duty defend his country. Signed up like Old Uncle Sam pointing his crooked finger at everybody said sign up. But the army lies. They don't want colored soldiers.

Treat us like slaves. Like animals. Yes they did. And nothing we could do about it. Behave like they say you better behave or they lock you in the stockade. Beat you, kill you quick as they kill the enemy we all spozed to be together in the U.S. Army to fight. Treat us colored soldiers like they own us, like they got the God-given right to kick us, spit on us and the only right we got is salute and say, Yes, sir. Here's my behind, sir. Kick it again, sir. Dirty dog duty or days we're mules and horses and elephants carrying Uncle Sam's war on our backs.

Don't you believe a word they putting out about Mr. Till, God rest his soul. Any the fellows went through the war, tell you what I'm telling you, Mrs. Till. Say just exactly what I'm saying. No different for colored over there in the war than things here today, in this United States of America. This Chicago. White man lie and say you're guilty—you're guilty. Case closed.

Now I'm not saying terrible things didn't happen in the war. But not just colored boys doing wrong. All the lies they put in the newspaper you'd think it was just us doing wrong. Just colored soldiers guilty. Not the truth, Mrs. Till. Never met your husband, but he was a soldier in the same colored army I served in, Mrs. Till. So the bad they say he did, maybe he did, maybe he didn't, but if the army say he did bad things, your husband finished. Never had a chance. Nothing a colored soldier can do about it. Nothing, Mrs. Till. Not until God rises up off His throne and stomps down those golden stairs and stops the lies.

Mamie Till wrote an autobiography. Didn't give Louis Till much space in it. According to Mrs. Till, Louis was often brutal with her. Put his hands on her. Then absent. Then dead. Then he turned up ten years later at a very inconvenient time, an embarrassing boogeyman from Mamie's past to haunt the trial of their son's murderers. Mamie wrote that Emmett was Louis Till's only accomplishment and in the end his only reason for being on earth. Must have been a bit more to her relationship with Louis than that, I believe. Probably adored the cute, mischievous little boy insidc her handsome, mean man Louis. Maybe a tough guy was attractive to her. Maybe she thought she could stick her head in the lion's jaws without getting hurt. Mamie also a down home, practical country girl. What sorts of men available in Argo, Illinois. What choices did she have. Most colored men and women newly arrived immigrants from the south, people marginalized economically, socially, in segregated enclaves. Mamie Carthan took a chance with Louis Till. Hoped she could tame him, mother him into a decent, dependable man. A project that was failing, she wrote. Then the army took Louis. Mamie Till probably lavished all her love on Emmett while she waited for Louis to return. After a telegram from the army said Louis Till dead, she could fall in love with him again in the person of his son. And this time love him without the worry of getting mauled.

Of course Mamie Till a lion, too. Like my mother she did not derive her sense of self-worth solely from her relationship with a son, though she would do anything in her power to protect him and demonstrate her love. If the Till offspring had been a daughter, Mamie Till would have loved her as much as she loved a Louis Till son. Like my mom, Mamie Till worked hard to maintain her integrity, dignity, honesty, her consistency in how she viewed herself, how she treated other people and expected them to treat her. Once I grew smart enough to appreciate my mother's example, I attempted to emulate her but fell far short of her standards.

Mamie Till, a lion and a warrior. She risked her life in September of 1955 when she traveled from Chicago to Mississippi. Her son Emmett's blood still fresh on the hands of the murderers she confronted at the trial in Sumner. Threats, harassment, disrespect did not chase her back to Chicago, though she admitted in her memoir she was deeply frightened each day by the ordeal of the trial, by cars that trailed the car she rode in from the courtroom to her motel, by bullets she lay in bed at night waiting to hear crash through the windows of her room. Soon after she returned home from Mississippi, she became a public spokesperson, a relentless witness who told her story to anyone willing to listen. First with NAACP officials sharing the podium as her sponsors, then alone, on her own two feet, traveling to welcoming cities or hostile cities across the country. She persisted in this work, until her death—speaker, writer, activist, dedicated crusader for civil rights, determined not to allow her fellow Americans to forget the terror, the injustice inflicted upon her son Emmett. Upon many, many other colored children of colored mothers.

Mamie Till remembers fixing Louis a sandwich. She wraps it in waxed paper, folds the edges like you gift wrap so edges even and neat. She's out of rubber bands. Rubber bands not around like before the war. Hopes the sandwich will hold together. Tucks it into a brown paper bag, adds an apple, creases the bag's top tightly shut. *What kind damn sammich dat.* She does not respond *What the hell damn kind do you think, Louis Till. A T-bone steak sammich,* hands ready to fly up to protect her face. No. Don't start. She is Louis Till's wife. Her mother's good daughter. Her daddy's sweet girl. Raised in Argo Temple Church of God in Christ. *Baloney,* she answers. A baloney sandwich for your lunch today, Louis. Thank goodness Louis not listening for an answer, not looking for a fight this morning. Brown bag in hand he's out the door. Slams it behind him. She can allow her arms to relax, her fists to drop to her sides. Wipe her fingers on her apron. Finish her thought. A baloney sandwich for your lunch break at Argo Corn Products, Louis, with my daddy and all the other colored men carrying *sammiches* fixed by wives, mothers, women who buy cold cuts from the A & P with money from Corn Products paychecks.

Baloney. Three paper-thin, pink slices between four slices of white bread. I wish like you wish Louis it could be country ham or turkey or roast beef or half a fried chicken with potato salad, greens and biscuits Louis but you know good and well Louis you only give me baloney money and plenty of times I don't even see baloney money. Do my best. Spread margarine on bread then mustard and mayonnaise, some ketchup if we have ketchup in the house. When I press the slices together, careful not to press too hard, and get the crusts messy. Wipe stuff from the knife back inside the bread so I don't waste. It's baloney today Louis not one of those mustard and mayonnaise days, so consider yourself lucky today, man, and yes I know you work hard Louis and I know you want more and I truly believe you deserve more and I know you think the only way you can get more is card playing and shooting dice Louis and you lose the little bit we have and you don't bother to come home at night like there's nothing here to come home to I guess you think Louis with the cupboard bare and my tired, bare face up in your face, my tears, my mouth all twisted up to holler at you when you come in here empty-handed and maybe you're shamed, maybe my tired body not enough for you, just good for scrubbing floors, washing your clothes, and even with everything I do around here to make a decent home Louis sometimes I believe it means nothing to you, home no place special in your mind, slinking in here with your hands empty when the money's gone and you can't even give me the little bit I need to feed you and feed myself so my body can feed my child, your child, Louis, our baby I carry every day God sends here and when you're not home I'm here day and night carrying your child Louis and today it's a baloney and bread *sammich* Louis and roll your big eyes at me if you need to but what else you think it's going to be.

I can hear you mock me down at Corn Products, see you ball up the paper I take my time to fold to make nice for you and hear you fuss at the sandwich I made and I wish wish maybe just once Louis you could try not to tear the wax paper, not crumple it up and toss it in the trash at work. I wish one day you would save wax paper I wrap your sandwich in. Why can't you for once just fold the wax paper up neatly like a person folds a nice letter to slip in an envelope and bring it back home in the bag and I could use bag and paper again and it would save a little money, Louis, but that's not the only reason why.

Little Mississippi. Mamie Till say it like she proud. Argo, Illinois, but we call it Little Mississippi, she say. So many of us from down there come up here to live. On Mama's street lots of family. Aunt Marie. Uncle Kid. June Bug. Uncle Crosby. Then next block it's Aunt Babe and Uncle Emmett and Great-Uncle Lee Greene. Mama and them started up Argo Temple Church of God in Christ and Sunday morning it's Webb, Mississippi, all over again right here in Argo.

Louis Till shuts his eyes to hide from her, hide what he's thinking. He ain't no country ass Webb ass Mississippi ass goddamn Negro. He shadowboxes. Speed bag blippety-blip-blip. Fists a blur. He's from Missouri not no goddamn lynch niggers Mississippi. Ain't no damn cotton fields out where he come from. Day he leaves New Madrid he looks through a dirty bus window at fields of something growing and truth is he don't know what the fuck it supposed to be. Maybe corn for Corn Products. Alagra syrup and Mazola cooking oil and margarine. Argo starch with that green and yellow Indian man on the box look like he a ear of corn. They make every damned thing from corn. Corn they grow out west and he sees flying green fields, flying Indian man boxes, flying speed bag. Opens his eyes, nods at this Mamie and hopes she's done talking that dumb country ass shit she's talking.

Asks his self why Mississippi Negroes never get enough of other Mississippi Negroes night or day. Sure won't ask her.

Everybody white as snow out in Missouri, Louis Till would like to say to Mamie if he could. But there are some Negroes out there because here he is black in Argo, Illinois, so got to be some black like me back in Missouri. She know the name of her people come up here, names of her people down there, all her people names and he don't know one, not one of his people. No names. Only Louis Till. Orphan. No middle initial. No people. What I'm spozed to do, girl, with all those names you saying. Not my names. Not my church. Not my people. Got none. Got one name, *Till.* Louis Till. Me. My people. My name.

Alma, my mama's name. Alma Gaines Carthan, Mrs. Till explains in her book, raised me close up under her so when I met Louis I was innocent about the world. Mama never talked to me about female things. Once a boy stole a kiss when we were playing in the school yard. Shook me up so much I ran straight to Mama when I got home from school. *Mama, I'm pregnant, Mama.* She's shook up, too, hugs me, both us crying. Then I tell her about the boy kiss me and she look at me like I'm crazy. Smacks me hard. *Whap.* Girl, you ain't pregnant. I don't stay dumb long but the way Mama raises me keeps me dumb long enough to think Louis Till real smart. Louis good looking and been out in the world on his own two feet his whole life so Louis seem to a girl like me like he knew just about everything. Swept me off my feet, you could say. Mama surprise me when she say *Yes* you may go with Louis Till to get ice cream. My first date with Louis. First date with anybody. A walk over to Kline's Deli and Ice Cream Parlor.

On the way to Kline's, Louis nice as could be, walking alongside me like a perfect gentleman and he asks me about this and that, you know. Louis never did talk much but there he is with his big-eyed, big, brown, good-looking self walking beside me asks me one or two little things, smiling like he likes to hear my answers and I'm chattering away I bet like some country bumpkin fool telling Louis Till all my business even though I didn't have no business to tell and he's not giving up a bit of his. But there I am pleased as a pea in a pod with a handsome young man strolling down the Argo streets. Sure hope somebody sees us. Running my big mouth and probably grinning way way too much, too. Chattering away like if I don't hurry up and say something make him fall in love with me before we get to Kline's, Louis be gone and I'd be Cinderella in the story when the clock strikes midnight.

Walking to Kline's with Louis my feet don't hardly touch the ground. Only thing I remember worrying me a bit was Louis asked me do I like banana split. Think to myself. *Banana split.* Why split. Louis work every day at Corn Products and a whole banana don't cost very much. Why we got to split one. If Louis really love me and wants me to marry him, why wouldn't Louis buy me my own banana. But I just smiled up at him and shook my head yes because one little bump don't ruin a ride. Half a banana, half a doughnut, half a peanut, anything Louis buy for me in Kline's fine with me. Any boy ever brought me anything, I ask myself. No the answer. Nothing. So shush, girl. If Louis Till buy a banana, and split it with you, take your half and say, Thank you so much, Louis.

Louis stepped right up to the counter at Kline's like he's been stepping up to counters his whole life. Said two banana splits. Mr.

Kline looks away from Louis and gives me one of his sneaky, half-way wanna be cute grins I never appreciated on his face when he tells me to tell Alma he said, *Hi.* Then he sets two brown, hard cardboard bowls on the counter. Picks two bananas off a yellow pile in front of sliding glass doors with every sort of shiny dish, bowl, glass, cup and saucer behind them you need to serve people in a nice soda fountain kind of place. Lays each banana in a bowl. Slices them long way down the middle. One scoop each of three different color ice creams, chocolate sauce over the ice cream, sprinkle of nuts, a long squirt of whipped cream last thing before a big red cherry on top. *Banana split.* So that's what Louis talking about. *Banana splits.*

Get you a take-out box and some dry ice so your ice cream don't melt before you get home, Mamie, Mr. Kline says and winks at me, but Louis picks up his bowl in one big hand, tells me with his eyes to pick mine up and follow him over to a booth under the window.

Now I know better than to sit down in Mr. Kline's store. Those red cushion stools at the counter and red booths under the front window for white customers not colored customers. Been knowing that's the way it is since the first day I come up to Argo from Webb with my mama to be with my daddy after he found work at Argo Corn Products. Seems like certain things you always knew or better know and nobody needs to tell you. Whether it's Webb, Mississippi, or up here in Argo, Illinois, if you're colored, certain things you understand and you better understand and best not forget. Even if you're an empty-head little girl your eyes and ears tell you certain things or maybe it's a rotten egg something in the air your nose smells. Point is, deep down you know better and know best not to take a chance going nowhere you're not supposed to be. Guess I was still floating, still daydreaming my Louis

Till fairy tale because I followed Louis and sat down across from him in the red cushion booth right under the window and had a spoonful of banana split halfway to my mouth before I looked up and there's Mr. Kline standing just where I knew he would be in the aisle at the end of the booth and he says exactly the words I knew he would say don't matter I'm with Louis Till or not.

You know youall can't eat in here, Mamie.

Louis not a particularly tall man. Seemed real tall to stumpy me, but Louis more what you'd call a big, strapping man. Big enough to be a tall handful if he stared at you in that way of his. Don't remember whether I put a spoonful of ice cream, banana, whipped cream, nuts and chocolate sauce in my mouth or set the plastic spoon back down in that cardboard bowl. Too scared to taste or swallow anyway when I see how Louis stared at Mr. Kline. Wanted to get up from that booth and run. Run home. Run, run, run to Mama fast as my legs could carry me.

Louis didn't say a word and neither did Mr. Kline. Louis just rolled his eyes slowly up the man's white apron to the man's red face. I watched those cold eyes of Louis and didn't see Mr. Kline go away but I knew he was gone. Never took my eyes off Louis and forgot all about running away.

So long before there was a Dr. King, had my own Dr. Martin Luther King. Before Louis went off to fight the war, had my very own warrior in Argo, Illinois. It was Louis and me that Saturday afternoon integrated Kline's Deli and Ice Cream Parlor. Sitting in the red window booth, Louis shining on me and I believe me shining on him while we ate those banana splits. Seemed like before long half of colored Argo paraded past peeking in at us to see if what they heard was true. Some of them got brave, start to come in, order a sundae, a soda and sit down, too. Whole place full of colored by the time I finished my very first banana split. Colored taken every seat and some standing around licking ice cream cones or just standing there to be there and be seen, and Kline's never went back to the way it was.

Mama mad at me. Mad at Louis Till for mixing her little girl up in foolishness that could have got us both killed. But what's Mama going to say. Louis was right. I think she liked Louis a little more after that. Even though she never would come right out and say it. I sure liked him more. More when I was already too much in love with him for my own good. Thought I had found a man who would never let anything bad happen to me. A man not scared. A big, strong man to protect me. Louis not especially tall, like I said, but he don't need to be tall. He used to shadowbox. *Shadowbox* what he called it once when I asked him what in the world was he doing, jump up like a crazy man all the sudden and go to prancing and dancing around Mama's living room, his big fists balled up, punches a mile a minute popping in the air, his head and shoulders herky-jerky like he's a puppet and somebody else crazy pulling the strings. *Shadowbox,* he said. I didn't understand a thing bout boxing but I knew nobody could stand up to Louis coming after them with both fists flying. Nobody else in the room, just Louis punching with both fists, but I knew Louis knocking down all the other boxers. *Bam. Bam.* One after another falling. Down they'd go and I'd want to clap and holler. Go on, Louis. Go, man. Me so proud and way too much in love. *Shadowboxing* he said.

* * *

Snow. Snow. Snow. Seems like some winters in Chicago snow every day. Wake up in the morning look out the window, see snow falling and think to myself, Huh-uh, Mamie. Can't be snowing again. Must be starch blowing over here from Argo Products. Big cloud of cornstarch making everything white. Tried to tell my cousins down in Webb, Mississippi, the summer I was twelve and visiting, about cold and snow up north. Not the little-bitty sprinkle of snow some of them had seen or chilly like it is when people down there talk about how cold it can get in Mississippi. No. No. No. Hey, youall. Listen up. Got a wind in Chicago call it Hawk. Hawk snatch you bald head. Nobody liable to see you ever again. And snow. Ima tell youall something about snow. In Chicago it snow, snow, snow every day. Higher than youall's house. Cars can't drive nowhere till snowplows big as a bus come and clean up. So much snow you can make a snowman tall as people. It's Frosty the snowman. Stones for eyes, stick for a nose. Another stick for a pipe.

My cousins standing round all google-eyed, hushed up for once till the oldest one, Clarence, cut his eyes at me and said, You lying, Mamie Till.

Tattle Tale Tit
Your tongue shall be split
Every dog in the town
Shall have a little bit

Louis Till sits shivering, chest bare, trousers wet, shirt drying over the back of one of Alma Carthan's kitchen chairs. Mamie scalded him good. He hollered like a stuck pig. Runned out the apartment. Never saw Mamie in the dark. Never saw black boiling water coming till it smack him. All up in the chest, his shoulder, splashes on his cheek. Felt like one side of him blew up all the sudden and blood burns, wet fire pouring down his arm, his chest. He howls. Down the steps, out on the pavement before he sees under a streetlamp it's not blood. Hot, hot damned water. Boiling, scalding hot. Why she got to do that. Out here burned up and dripping wet in the goddamned street where's he spozed to go. It's little Mississippi, she said, and niggers love being up under other niggers sure enough and he runs all soaking black blood, wet black skin falling off to Mother Carthan's door. Where else he gon go.

She looks across a chain that keeps the open door locked. *Dat you. Dat you dere, Louis Till.* Why it take her all that long studying through the cracked-open door to see it's him. She know good and damn well who. He shakes now. Grits his teeth so they don't chatter. Nothing to say anyway. What he spozed to say. Say to Mamie's mama Mamie did it. Scalded him. Skin hurts under the wet shirt maybe the wet is blood after all. Your crazy girl did it, Mother Carthan. Open the goddamn door. Stares at his wet shoes. Waits. Hurts. Waits. Hears the chain slide. *That you, Louis Till. My Mamie all right, Louis Till.* Don't she see it's him standing there at her door bleeding to death. It ain't Mamie on fire she sees at her door, damnit. It's him, half his chest blowed off. Ain't nothing wrong with Mamie except the bitch crazy. She ain't the one hurt bad, she the one done the scalding.

Sit down, Louis Till, her mama say. Get out that wet shirt. Easy, easy does it, boy. My, my. What you two been doing. You sit still here. Got to telephone my poor baby.

Mamie says butter. Margarine if you don't have butter. Butter cool the burning. Butter help heal, she say. Say tell him stay away from me, Mama. Don't ever want to see you again, Louis, her mama say Mamie said. Stay away, Mamie says.

He stops Mamie in front of the hardware store. Right down from Kline's. What she need in the hardware store. What the hell she know how to fix.

Leave me alone, Louis. You can't follow me around and bother me like this. Judge said don't bother me. Don't even come near me the court paper says and here you are dogging me like a shadow. I know Louis Till doesn't give a damn what I say or anybody else says. But it's the law this time telling you to leave me be. You best go on away from me, Louis. Don't block my way, man.

(. . .)

Don't you dare touch me. Don't want your hands on me ever again. And I mean it. You had your chance. Lots and lots of chances, Louis Till. Too many chances. Too late now. It's over now. Finished. Just leave me alone.

(. . .)

Let me by, Louis. People watching, Louis. Stop before you get yourself in deep trouble.

(. . .)

You just don't understand do you. And you never will. We have nothing to say to each other. Just step back so I can go about my business.

(. . .)

Please.

(. . .)

Don't make me hate you. It doesn't have to be ugly like this.

Don't make trouble, Louis. I'm sorry, Louis. Truly sorry. For you and me. For poor little Emmett. But it's over now. Let it go, Louis. No more trouble, please.

(. . .)

I'm awful weary of seeing you here, Mr. Till. I could cite you for contempt, lock you up, and then I wouldn't have to see you in my courtroom for a good long while. But given the national emergency, I'm going to offer you an option. Rather than becoming a burden to Illinois taxpayers, you can serve your country, Mr. Till. Go down the hall and enlist in the United States military. Today. Immediately, Till. Or off to jail with you. Which will it be, Mr. Till. Army or prison.

OVERSEAS

My father, who served in the United States Army same years Louis Till served, told me that some Sunday mornings before dawn they'd blow a bugle inside the colored soldiers' barracks. Roust our bad, no-sleep heads. Bugle call and everybody still stinking drunk, still asleep, half-destroyed, half-dressed, guys throw up, guys knock each other out the way to get in line and get out of line, scramble back inside the barracks to piss a quick piss, quick runny shit. All us mad, lined-up and bleary-eyed, clothes slept in, fought in, danced in, bled in, punch-ups, vomit in the street outside the club last night. Shit. A sure enough sorry bunch of colored GIs, lemme tell you, he said. My father said, talkative a minute about his army days. Sunday morning, he said, and you might think the bugle call a damned go to church call, but not church on those Georgia crackers' minds. Slaves on their mind. They say you guilty of some bullshit or another they slave your ass. Slave you to a peckerwood farmer for a week or put you on the road gang. And this ain't 1844. It's damn 1944. Damn Savannah, Georgia, in the good ole U.S. of A. and we're in Uncle Sam's uniform fighting Uncle Sam's war, but believe it or not, sonny boy, that's how they did us down there.

If Louis Till had been around to school his son Emmett about the south, about black boys and white men up north and down south, would Emmett have returned safely from his trip to Money, Mississippi, started up public high in Chicago that fall of 1955, earned good grades like I did, eluded the fate of his father, maybe even become successful and rich. President of the United States. But the flame of his father's fate draws Emmett like a moth. Son flies backward and forward simultaneously like the sankofa bird because part of the father's fate is never to be around to protect, advise, and supervise his son, the fate of father and son to orphan each other always. Fathers and sons. Sons and fathers. An eternal cycle of missing and absence. Bright wings flutter like a dark room lit suddenly by a match.

In the nursing home, the veteran, my father, also said—his speech a surprise each time he speaks, always in his street voice, his polite waiter's voice long gone—losing something, not the worst thing in the world. Losing something means you had something to lose. Means some fool get up in your face and say, *you ain't nothing, nigger,* you can frown at the fool or smile or smack the fool upside the head if he persists in his foolishness. Pay him no mind my father said cause you got the memory of the good thing and nothing nobody says till the day you die can take that away.

I traced Till's outfit, Company 177 of the 379th Battalion, Transportation Command, from Casablanca to Civitavecchia to Naples. Beyond the bare facts of their deployments, I couldn't discover much concerning their activities or whereabouts. Probably about as much as colored soldiers of the 379th knew in 1944. Transport Command troops pack up and ship out when officers bark commands. Private Louis Till winds up in the rubble of another town he's never heard of, never imagined, orphan again, and he will stay there as long as officers say stay.

Sometimes, Private Louis NMI (no middle initial) Till, 36392273, of 177 Port Company, 379th Battalion, T.C., must know he's in Italy. Knows it don't make no fucking difference but he knows sometimes. Knows it well as he knows his own name, *Louis Till.* As well as he knows the number 2 plus the number 0 equals his age—20—when he enlisted. And knows he's not going to get much older. And so what. Age ain't nothing but a number. Don't mean a thing. Nothing. Not a got-damned thing. Knows he's Louis Till and grown, been grown, and he's in one place today, tomorrow another place maybe, another city or town, another no place in the middle of no where and so what. He's Louis Till. Him. Everything he always is. He knows his name, age, color, a nigger, a orphan so why he got to say it out loud every day. No need to be walking around like he's afraid he might forget name, rank, serial number and what belongs to him in the ditty bag up under his goddamn bunk in the goddamn camp in this goddamn country. Why he need to go around saying shit if he knows shit. He knows he's a grown man and been grown since way back as long as he can remember, since back in New Madrid, Missouri, that day he sees a black boy on a fold-up, pissy cot crying like a baby and he's a grown man in the doorway, Louis Till grown up already, eight years old watching hisself cry and he hollers, Why don't you shut the fuck up. Hush your sorry-ass mouth, nigger, nobody listening to you, nobody care nothing bout you crybaby motherfucker why don't you just shut the fuck up. Why you sitting there in broad daylight, a grown-ass man in short pants sitting on a rock with his big head in his hands crying funny, crying like a baby pissed his bed. You ain't no child, you a damn grown man, fool. Why don't you shut up, sitting alongside the road everybody goes up to get that vino man you lucky I ain't crossed-over and smacked you off that rock, nigger, in them raggedy pieces of uniform they all wear creeping through here now the United States Army finished kicking they dago asses good. Sneaking home and crying funny like a bitch. Who the fuck he think he is with his funny little cap about to fall off his big grown man head. Crying funny just like they talk funny and got that funny money over here ain't worth shit, a wheelbarrow full ain't worth nothing don't make no sense and so what, Private Till thinks, long as he can talky-talky him up some vino and talky-talk him up some pussy him talking funny like them and they talking funny like niggers when they wants something niggers got and that's how Private Till knows it's Italy.

"Night in Tunisia." Did Louis Till know the tune. Could Till hear it as his ship approached North Africa. The song floats in the air, plays itself to be heard, passed on. Did Louis Till smile, whistle the music, though the tune was not written down, not playing on records or radio at the time. Does he smile at the fact he lands in a North African city full of brown people and black people that goes by the name Casablanca, *white house.*

A guidebook would inform Louis Till if he cared to consult one, that in 1468 the Portuguese attacked Anfa, a Berber settlement dating back to the seventh century, captured the town and later developed it to serve as a port, Casablanca, in a rapidly expanding network of imperial commerce founded upon, then flourishing through the buying and selling of African bodies. Today Anfa is a shopping center in sprawling Casablanca. Louis Till could read this in another book and read in yet another that when approached by ship, the city's an idea, whitewashed ramparts and white mazes of low square dwellings, row after row terraced on piggybacked hills that slope gently to the water. He could read how the gleaming whiteness creates mirages, dreams, phantoms on the horizon and when the sky is clear, the city is doubled in the water like blue sky's doubled by the deep blue ocean upon which you sail, gliding, skimming over the waves, bobbing in the chop, then glide again, slower, slowly as sea flattens and the ship draws closer to what appears to be a single immense dwelling that sprawls on the hills, *Casablanca,* a white house built of sun-bleached, sun-polished bones from which dark flesh has vanished.

Louis Till leafs through invisible pages, listens to invisible words to find what he needs to know (for instance, women in Casablanca are divided by color, not necessarily by the color of their skins but by the color of the troops they hang with, the ones who go with colored boys and the ones who don't, a color line policed here absolutely, brutally, ruthlessly as the color line at home, so beware, my man, of white helmets, white armbands, white puttees, flying squads of white MPs in jeeps who enforce the local color code, and punish unmercifully, gleefully, with lead-lined batons, white-gloved fists, steel-toed boots, with cocked 45s and barbed-wire stockades all colored offenders who dare cross the line), a guidebook of stories Louis Till and his colored buddies knew well, stories told by guys who have been to Casablanca or guys repeating lore passed down a thousand years by successive waves of colored soldiers, slaves, seamen, passing through, awaiting cargoes, repairs, provisions or stationed here or stalled like Odysseus before the walls of Troy in *The Golden Book of Greek Myths* my mother read to me.

War is mostly rumor and myth for men in the Transportation Command, colored men like Louis Till and just about every other colored soldier because with very few exceptions, I learn, colored are assigned to Transport Command service units and seldom see with their own eyes war like in the movies. No firefights, bayonet duels, no huddling in a foxhole, no comrades falling, blown up beside you as you charge across a field, everybody shooting and shouting like in a colored director's movie I had rented recently about colored combat troops in Italy in World War II. No. The Transport Command's war a rumble of distant guns, distant cities burning at night on the horizon. War most real for colored soldiers when they bury white guys, young guys far from home like them.

* * *

On rare days, rare nights war lets Louis Till get fucked up. Get his head bad, punch niggers, buy pussy, fuck up good if he's listened to stories passed down from colored soldier to colored soldier, learned to follow maps drawn in air of invisible cities, deeper cities within cities where war lands him. Second cities he'll know by their touch, smell, sound. You see them only if you know how to look. In this white house *Casablanca* a market hides, nigger market blacker than the white folks' blackest market is what Louis Till hears and in that market he can sell cartons of Camels he steals from truckloads he steals for white officers. American cigarettes colored guys say he can trade for a silver ring with his initials on it and *Casablanca, 1943.* I watch Louis Till scratch letters in the sand. He watches an Arab whose face under a brown hood is darker than his, pound L.T. into the ring with quick, precise strokes.

The one they call *Saint*—what the fuck else they spozed to call a negro named Louis who comes from Missouri—stumbles from the crowd of other sweaty colored men, wobbly, dizzy on his feet, a windup woogie just about danced itself to death. He wobbles out the mess out there where no room to dance, it's war out there, people bump and grab and knock. People hold on to people's arms to get past, to get through. You nod, and they nod and grapple, cling, wrestle. You hang on and rub and get smacked apart, flung together. Some garlic breath bitch all up in your face you rub her big behind, hold on till some nigger call hisself dancing snatch her fling her, she gone. Hair short as a man's and shoulders broad as a man and big farm girl hand can squeeze hard as you can squeeze and you push a knee, a thigh into her meat. Rub, touch Miss Ann soft hair. Rub a leg up in there and she grinds she bounces away another fool got her, and gone.

Saint. Over here, Saint. Over there's the table, McMurray, Kitchen, Junior Thomas, Hite. Glass of beer in each of Till's hands, quick hands don't shake, break you up. Here he come sipping both glasses, Till ain't carrying no beer for none those fools at the table, Till fight you try to take one of his half-full, half-empty glasses. Here he come bumping to the table, nerve to call hisself dancing, halfway falls, a fucking war out there man *fiky-fiky* work bitch fuck you through your clothes right out there under that red light in the ceiling. Work bitch, work. Hey man how you doing, man, hey blood, hey splib, hey spook, hey home watch the fuck where you're going nigger yeah man you my man kick your ass, fool, cool breeze, be spades, be coons, be your brother man, hey, hey, man watch the fuck out the way, man, that's my man, Saint. *Say hey, all the way,* it's the 177 of the 379, shit yeah. *Say hey, Saint.* Gotta be okay.

Louis Till finishes both glasses of beer before he reaches the table. Eyes big as saucers, eyeballs rolling round like he's checking to make sure the room's where it was before he blinked. He's coming up for air, born again, remembering instantly the presence of ancient enemies. There's beer down the front of his khaki blouse. Beer in his fists slopping out so he can't bob and weave and duck, can't counterpunch, hook, clinch. No footwork, no feint, slip, jook. You run, skip, hop-hop-hop for hours, days, months in the gym to go a quick minute in the ring. Why you go through all that dumb shit, man—why you waste your time, man. Look like some big old wobbly bear on a bicycle stumbling over here from the bar. You crazy, Till. Sit your behind down, boy. Before you fall down. Nobody gone pick your big black ass up off the floor if you fall, boy. Sit your drunk self down, Saint, before you fall down, Saint.

He didn't live long enough to hear Otis Redding sing "Dock of the Bay" and Otis didn't live very long either, but since Louis Till *knows there*, you could say he *goes there*, sits on a dock at the edge of the bay, stares at the sea he hears more clearly than sees. It's night, no stars. Now and then a flash way, way out, the sudden white sheen of a wave's marcelled crown etched a second before it crashes into another wave, black wave after wave invisible if no shine blinks here and there, blinks like somebody searching, combing the black sea with a flashlight beam.

He's on the dock of a bay and listens to far-off waves explode like big guns and smaller, closer waves lap and suck the sea, it's very near indeed, sloshes inside his belly, though sea also distant as the Casablanca moon hidden by clouds tonight after a whole day of white sky and white heat and humping ammo boxes with McMurray, Thomas and Hite. Sky black now but he recalls sun on his back, and remembers a pinkish, freckle-faced boy in New Madrid, orphan like him, nigger like him, name gone, but round, pale face comes back clear as a bell, the pigeon-face boy with a sliver of eyeglass in his speckled pink hand, showed him how you burn holes in newspaper. Glass makes fire like a match, a tiny white circle hotter and hotter, then a curl of smoke and the paper burns. Burns like Till's dark skin in Italy's white niggerish heat.

Till wished he had eyes in the back of his head. He could watch his self catch fire. Would a twist of smoke rise, like from that bug his quick hand snatched and pulled off the wings. Then they cooked it, wriggly legs wriggle faster, faster. Black bug on its back going nowhere.

No eyes back there. No sun. No moon. Silent black sky, noisy black sea. On the dock of the bay he hears Otis. Hears wood creak. Wooden posts in the water hold up one end of the dock where he sits. Legs dangle, heels touch nothing when he swings them. Lets the thought come into his mind of the whole damn dock a chair one of them fools snatches out from under him and his crew laughs at the look on ole Till's face. Saint Till from dry-ass Missouri drops into the sea and he don't know a lick about swimming. Till would laugh too, if he had time before he drowns. Pretty funny if he thought about it. Dumb arms and legs trying to learn to fly, learn to swim, before he hits the water. Funny even if it's him, his turn.

Everybody laughing. McMurray got the biggest mouth. Laughs loudest. Damned greedy-ass McMurray on the dock behind him tonight. McMurray got lucky. Heads you lose, tails I win, Till. Talked that silly old shit but he got lucky, goes first. Big mouth McMurray back there in those boxes, getting him some trim. All up in them Miss Ann drawers. McMurray got lucky goes first. You called *tails*, Till. You lose, Till. What else he spozed to call. It's about *tail*, right. *Tails wrong.* Wrong, you wrong, Till. Wrong. *Heads.* My turn first. And Ima wear that trim out. Shut up, nigger, and hurry up, nigger, we ain't got all night. Hurry up, McMurray, you ain't nothing, just got lucky, nigger. Hurry up. Over and out, nigger. I ain't sitting here waiting on no goddamn dock of the bay the whole damn night. One more minute, I'm coming back there snatch you off it, nigger. My Johnson tired of listening to you. You ain't nothing no way, nigger. Just lucky. Just get up off it. You know you ain't doing nothing.

POET

Private Louis Till, incarcerated in the Mediterranean Theater of Operations, United States Army (MTOUSA) Disciplinary Training Center, Metato, Italy, must have wondered what kind of motherfucker so bad they weld steel bars to his cell. Old skinny white motherfucker army gon hang, they say. Poet, they say. Dry as a dried up rattlesnake skin. In a cage with extra bars they say cause he badder than a nigger, they say. Till thinks, *No-no. Huh-uh, No damn way.* Rolls his eyes, sucks his teeth, hisses *Shee-it* at nobody in particular, shakes his head *no* and says *shee-it* again under his breath. No goddamn way. These motherfuckers nuts round here.

A traitor they call him. Poet Ezra Pound convicted by his own treasonous words. Betrayed his country on the radio. Friend of the enemy. Off with his poet's head. Confined until trial in what he dubbed *my gorilla cage*, in duplicate letters, one posted to his sweetheart wife, one to his mistress. Witnesses agree Pound suffered. Alone night and day in a bare, outdoor, steel-barred, steel-mesh-reinforced, roofless cell. Some say it broke him, say he drooled, barked, chased his tail. Many observers believed and continue to believe the poet deserved worse. Deserved more punishment than wind, sand, sun that cured his skin the parchment color of pages of Provençal ballads and lays he had read in a

Florence library. Hang the poet because he never learns. Continues to accuse. Blame. Excoriate. Deny. Complain like Sibyl singing in her cage.

One moonless night not long before they transferred him from a colored barracks to a locked death row isolation cell, two cells away from the poet Pound's cell, Private Till risks a beating or a bullet from guards who shoot to kill after curfew. Other colored prisoners know he sneaks out. *You crazy, Till,* somebody says. Till, falsetto, mocks him. *You crazy, Till.* Till grins at the others. Can't nobody hurt me. Dead man already.

Till knows he's lying through his teeth. A beating worse than a bullet to the brain. Hurts so bad he wants to cry like a baby. After the guards finish, blood, sweat and pus stick him to his cot. Hurts to breathe. Cuts sting like a swarm of angry bees. He sneaks out anyway every chance he gets. Breaks rules because if a prisoner doesn't break the rules, rules break your heart, my brother, my son, all the colored prisoners I know and have read about assure me.

Black sky drops like a hood over Till's whole body first step away from the barracks. Lights are strung on the fence like it's Christmas, but they can't change the darkness. Creep, creep. He pretends he's a spook nobody can see. Nobody wants to see. His feet know the invisible camp. Creep, creeps. Charmed, he believes under the dark, heavy hammer of sky. Nothing to lose, dead already, just one life and they took it, can't steal it again. A ghost already with a ghost wife, ghost son, ghost home in a ghost city, Chicago. But one night a voice calls out, *Till. Saint Louis Till.* Stopped in his tracks, he shivers. Hot as it was that particular night. Frozen absolutely still. Not a sound, not a breath. He's dead. Why another ghost fucking with him. Don't make no goddamn sense. Crazy fucking camp got me nuts, he thinks. Remembers the skinny, old white man. Death-row cages like shark teeth out there in the dark. Over there. Can't see shit, but sure enough a voice from over there. *Till.* Old white man with your name in his evil mouth. How the fuck he know your goddamn name, Till.

Doc. Do you think you could arrange for me to speak with one of my fellow guests. Private Louis Till. A nigger the niggers call Saint Louis. We might have been neighbors once. Back in Missouri. We're neighbors again here, so to speak. I'd love to chat with that particular colored boy before I'm transferred. A meeting with Private Till before the army hangs one or both of us.

Pater Dear and Mater Dear, the poet wrote his parents . . . 4 conditions necessary for a nation to produce an epic. Unfortunately, in our sweet land of liberty, none of the 4 exist. (1) a beautiful tradition (2) unity in the outline of that tradition, (3) a hero, mythical or historical (4) a damn long time for the story to lose all its garish detail and get encrusted with beautiful lies.

In spite of all the above, your humble son is trying his hand at epic. A modern epic must be a prose poem, I reckon. Mine will consist of three sections. The first will introduce a character who endures the meanest of lives. A nigger or slave, maybe. Part two will chronicle his miraculous transformation. Aided by pluck, luck and the gods' insatiable appetite for a good joke, the protagonist will achieve undreamed of success. From a life of no meaning wrest meaning. The third section will demonstrate the folly of meaning, the folly of abandoning irresponsibility. We will observe our hero (darky?) yearn unto death to taste again the sweet chaos of nothingness he's forsaken.

In his cell the poet listens to colored prisoners talk. Colored prisoners who speak a different language. Theirs is almost like his. His almost like theirs. He pilfers. Collects. Savors. Mimics. Envies their speech. His poet's fancy delighted, instructed by colored exchanges, colored words, colored names. Colored soldiers whose actual names are colors—Black. Green. Niggers bearing stolen names of white presidents—Washington. Jefferson. Wilson. They call Louis Till, *Saint.* In the poet's cantos Till is called a ram. He lends Till a greek god's name. Tags Till with a Chinese pictograph signifying negation, *-no, not.*

A poem by a colored poet, Robert Hayden, remembers names of slave ships—*Desire, Estrella, Amistad, Esperanza*—names he calls *bright, ironical . . . jests of kindness.*

The dark ships move, the dark ships move, Hayden wrote. Colored people like him cargo aboard those dark ships, dark cargo branded with new names. Old names lost. Silenced. Like Till's. Like mine. Old names forgotten before we discovered how to speak them.

Voyage through death to life upon these shores. Death, life, darkness, light too ancient to be owned by human beings of any color.

How many meanings and jests are imprisoned in *Till,* the traitorous poet Pound may have wondered as he unpacked meanings and jests in his own. Till (noun) a box for money. Till (verb) to prepare earth for seeds. Till (adverb/preposition?) a measure of time. How much time. Whose time. What is the weight of a pound of flesh. How much time left for Till, for him, the poet, fellow prisoner in the Metato, Italy, D.T.C. Till tried, convicted, doomed now to solitary confinement until he's hanged by the neck and dead. Until he's not Till. Till his time up. No time. Not a man. Why does the poet brand Till with all these names. Mark him *Otic*, ancient greek for *no one, nobody.* A name Ulysses named himself to fool the blind Cyclops.

Goodbye for now, my love. I miss you terribly, the poet writes to his wife and to his mistress. Pity your poor old Xerxes in his pointy cap and pointy beard, his magnificent armada wrecked by storms before it could conquer the Greeks. Yesterday the world's most powerful monarch. Today hiding in his tent, weeping.

Louis Till likes the idea of a fast, clean knockout. Finish off a guy. Get it over slick and quick. *Blam.* Hands not stinging not bleeding or busted up when you unwrap the tape. Sing that little song nobody hears you sing but you. Little tune inside your head when you finish something just the way you spozed to finish and it's done, finished, clean. *Uh-huh. Shee-it.*

He could sit like a dog or cat sit and watch all day all night the way that water come up and go back down the beach like water's one thing and wants to be another thing like maybe water wants to be land and water keeps coming up to land, climbs all over land but water ain't land it's water and land just sits there being land don't move a inch it's land like before water come up and still land after water go away and water still water no matter how many times it creep up on land all that water out there still water why it come back again to land when it just gon touch land and go back again to water long as you sit here and watch.

PITTSBURGH

Towards the end of the summer of 1955 I saw in *Jet* magazine a scary photo of a dead boy almost exactly my age, a dead colored boy murdered in Money, Mississippi, whose mutilated face looked like a black bug somebody had squashed under his thumb. I fell in love and had my heart broken the first time that same summer, but the big news on our end of Copeland Street, where a few raggedy houses held a few poor colored families living just down the block from Walnut Street's upscale shops, was neither my aching heart nor the far-off Mississippi murder of Emmett Till who we whispered about like it was our fault, a shameful, dirty secret. The big news that summer was a showroom fresh, three-tone green Mercury docked alien as a spaceship at the curb on our end of the block.

Like everybody else colored on the street I couldn't get enough of the spit-shined, fighter-jet sleek car. Its owner, Big Jim the gambler, who people said paid cash he won on a single roll of the dice for his new car, had given us another thing to talk about earlier in the summer. He started to appear, Brooklyn Dodgers cap on his head, baseball bat in hand at an early morning hour when nobody expected to see night owl Big Jim up and about on the street. Then all summer he bragged about how he caught a trolley car and went downtown every morning. Bragged that he planted his huge behind on a chair just inside the door of the Duquesne Light Company office. Scowling, bat across his knee, not saying a word till finally some office chump scared or tired or both of seeing him sitting there each morning asked what he wanted, sir, and in no uncertain terms, he told the person *Lights, dammit*, and Duquesne Light turned his lights back on that they'd turned off for lack of payment.

With a Big Jim scowl in his voice my father hollers from the kitchen: Get your tail in here, boy. Why didn't you come in the house when your mother called you last night.

Wasn't late, Daddy. Not hardly past ten o'clock.

Didn't ask you what the damn time was. Don't care what hour of night or day, when your mother tells you do something, you know you better do it. And quick.

She called me out the window. I wasn't nowhere, Daddy. Just sitting downstairs right across the street in Big Jim's car where Mom could see me if she looked.

Since when you grown enough to be sitting around at night in anybody's car.

Wasn't going nowhere, Daddy.

Then what you two doing in the damned car.

Nothing.

What he say to you.

Nothing, Daddy.

Well, I'll be talking to Mr. Big Jim soon's I get home from work tomorrow. Meanwhile, you're grounded. Don't set your foot out the door without asking your mother. And if she says yes, don't you even think about going anywhere near that lard-ass yellow man or his shit green car.

Three-tone green. Three colors were a fad that summer. All kinds of brand-new shiny rides in crazy color combinations dazzled the streets. Though for years most of us at the tail end of Copeland would continue to watch TV in black and white on small screens, picture snowy, flip-flopping, in 1955 we could peer through a Walnut Street appliance store window at a World Series tinted in wobbly colors on a twenty-one-inch Magnavox console.

Color's the future. Emmett Till's black and white photo in *Jet* the past, an old story of old-timey, terrible shit white men did to black boys down south. Changes coming fast but some things don't change. A long time after that summer of '55 and I'm still trying to make precise sense of my deep fear, my father's deep anger, my own deep anger, my father's deep fear, strutting peacock cars, fathers and sons afraid of each other. War and hate and terror and love.

On Copeland Street, Latreesha's pretty face arrived two months before the crushed face of Louis Till's son greeted me in *Jet* magazine. Same summer I see the photo of Emmett Till's dark face with all the boy, all the human being battered out of it, I'd fall in love the first time. Make love, so to speak, for the first time. With Latreesha. Sweet, sweet, impossibly pretty-faced, smooth-limbed, *Latreesha*. My first time in love and I'm gloriously loved back and then she's lost in a minute after I thought she would be mine forever. Latreesha's gone, never comes back, never another summer visit from New York City, never cuddles again with me on my grandmother's sofa. Only that once. One chance, Latreesha. We pass on the street, lovemaking not two weeks old, and she looks away, or worse, ignores me, grins like a Chessy cat at a guy who strolls beside her, arm round her shoulders, her eyes smiling up at him like he's the only person on planet earth. Latreesha long gone before she catches a Greyhound at the end of August back to New York City. Cruises past all summer in some dude or another's shiny ride, smiling, going places a fourteen-year-old chump with no wheels, no driver's license could take her. July and August she might as well be in Harlem where she came from before she arrived to stay the summer in my grandmother's house where Latreesha's father boarded on the first floor. He worked double shifts on his good job in the steel mill and Latreesha didn't know anybody else in town her age so I got my chance. She's my first love on the downstairs sofa bed in my grandmother's house while her daddy worked and Grandma snored like gangbusters upstairs.

Latreesha's visit and Emmett Till's murder were the same treacherous summer, each boxed in a separate set of memories and associations until it dawns on me that they shared 1955.

Latreesha showed up in June, the summer of Big Jim and his baseball bat in the Duquesne Light Company office, summer of the three-tone green car Big Jim bought with cold cash, summer of color TV in a store window, a summer ending in September with Emmett Till dead in darkest Mississippi. The rest of my life undreamed, a life that's much closer to over now, everything it was, is, and everything left to come, compressed into a space too small to imagine unless a name, a moment drops like a stone in a still pool and I'm the plummeting stone, the hole, the rings rippling, expanding, disappearing.

I couldn't get enough of Latreesha, her bright, sassy eyes, those very shapely little arms, strong and tough as a boy's she bragged, balling up her fist with pink polish on the nails to make a muscle she dared me to squeeze. Go on, chicken . . . can't hurt me. And sure enough that small girl wiped me out, opened my nose, broke and ate my heart during a summer that had seemed paradise the first weeks of June, my birth month. Emmett Till's last June alive. I may have made love the first time on my birthday. It could have happened on June 10, though not likely. Wouldn't the coincidence have been unforgettable. Let's just say to make this a good story, it could have been that precise day, a June 10 birthday present on the fold-out sofa and I've simply forgotten the date like I misplace the name *Latreesha* sometimes. Like I couldn't hold on to Latreesha and lost her forever. My bad habit of forgetting things, losing things, even precious things, getting worse as I grow older.

By the end of the summer I could pretend to laugh about Latreesha. Listen to Big Jim make fun of her in his car. He said that little peanut got the nerve to come switching her narrow fanny round here. Batting her eyes at me and I'm old enough to be her granddaddy. *Sure is a pretty car, Mr. Jim. You ever give rides to people in your pretty green car, Mr. Big Jim.* Women ain't shit, boy. Just out for what they can get.

Good to hear Big Jim say what I couldn't say out loud, couldn't even think inside myself. Not quite. Not yet. Not sure I really believed a word he said about Latreesha but I spent hours in that Mercury because I needed to hear it. Knew from a distance when he was inside the car because its belly dipped down closer to the street. Car's interior, shades of green to match the exterior, smelled like Henderson's Barbershop. Hair tonic, shaving lotion, the stinging, medicated cream Mr. Henderson or one of his sons pats on your neck when a haircut's finished, towel snapped off your shoulders. Henderson's what it smelled like when I sat on green leather upholstery beside Big Jim, and he riffed nonstop about every damned body, every damned thing. Stuff in the neighborhood, in the newspapers, on radio and TV. His talk like the barbershop when it's full of men signifying and telling lies, ball game loud on the radio, quiet gimpy Clement busy pushing his broom.

I used any excuse to go in Henderson's and listen to the men. If no ball game on, nobody's errand on deck to run, I'd loaf around outside with my cut buddies, our corner only a couple storefronts away from the barbershop. We couldn't catch voices inside Henderson's, but we could learn rhymes the old heads recited outdoors while they stood around laughing and teasing each other, or sat on boxes, or leaned back on chairs under the red letters of Henderson's window.

Oh, she jumped in bed
Pulled the covers over her head
And said I could not find her
Said yes I shall you silly gal
And jumped in bed behind her
She grabbed my goose
Wouldn't turn it loose
Stuck it in her

Coffee grounder
Feel the egg
Running down her leg
She know damn well
I found her

No way was I about to repeat those kinds of toasts to my father. No way I'd tattle on the nasty talk in Big Jim's car. Big Jim did most of the talking. In the dark that smelled like Old Spice and Watkins hair oil I did the listening. Thought all the time about Latreesha, but I couldn't say out loud how good it felt to hug that girl my mother tagged *fast.* I wanted to brag to somebody about copping pussy at barely fourteen. Didn't dare, because deep down I knew dumb luck was the only reason I copped and if I hoped to get that lucky ever again in life, best keep my mouth shut. My Latreesha story turned pretty pitiful, pretty quick, anyway. So good once, then so much hurt, shame, disappointment. Day after day I tried to figure out what I'd done wrong. Meanwhile I listened to Big Jim laugh at everybody's bonehead doings and ugly mugs and funky underwear. Watched Big Jim scowl when he said fuck those motherfucking evil white folks at Duquesne Light. Everybody's business in Big Jim's mouth like it's his job to drive the streets all day and spy on people so he could park his fancy car in the evening on the colored end of Copeland and sit at the curb until a boy like me with nothing better to do comes along and climbs in to hear all the bullshit Big Jim collected. A lonely, lovesick boy ready to sit and listen all night if he didn't have to be home before ten.

Latreesha. How could I forget her. I didn't. More like I filed her. Buried Latreesha's file. Afraid to put the pieces of that summer of '55 together. To make of it what. The summer I fell crazy in love before summer hardly got started. The summer that ends with the picture of a dead colored boy's face too terrible to look at.

Summer of a punch that landed my father in jail overnight. Your father's not hurt, my mother said. He's fine, they told me. Cut Jim Saunders up pretty bad, they said. Police took them both. Big Jim to the emergency room. Your daddy down to the precinct. One of the men said, Don't worry. Your husband be home this evening, tomorrow afternoon the latest. Big Jim bloody but ain't hurt bad, he told me. Said too much blubber on Jim before you get down to anything you could hurt bad. Said cops couldn't care less about two niggers fighting in the street. You know the cops. Put your husband in a cell to cool off. Couldn't really call it much of a fight, they told me. More like your father had decided to give Big Jim Saunders a whipping. You know your father's good with his hands from that little bit of boxing he used to do.

I can see my father shadowboxing. *Whomp. Whomp.* Punches in flurries. Punches too close for comfort graze air inches from my face, my mother's face. Louis Till. Bip. Bip. Bippiddy-bip. Weaves and bobs, turns Big Jim in circles, then sidesteps and an uppercut. *Whomp.* All the air flies out Big Jim's soft gut. My father marked him. Split his lip. Bloody nose. Eye swole up. Big Jim never had a chance. Bloody mess in a minute. Like the bull after a bullfighter wears his big ass out.

What could I say to my father about Mr. Big Jim's car. Problem was my father had needed to ask. Something about his fourteen-year-old son in a car at night with Big Jim my father could not trust. I heard distrust in my father's voice and never exactly trusted him again.

Hated him, the daddy I loved, when he told Rakhim, Don't plea-bargain. Don't admit you did something you didn't do. Tell the truth, Son. They can take a lot of things from you, but don't let them steal the truth. I know you didn't shoot that white boy, Rakhim. In my heart I know it sure as I'm standing here. Sure as I'm your father and black. Don't let them make you say you did that crime they say you did. Tell the truth, Son. Lawyer we got you a good lawyer. No case, he says. Nothing on you, Rakhim, unless you give them something.

And Rakhim, poor, unlucky Rakhim, said no plea bargain and does the time to disprove your point, Daddy. Oh, my good black man, Daddy. Lover man, loser man, Oh, my good, honest, cheating father. The dead victim was white, Daddy. Witness said a black man shot him. That's everything they needed to lock up my brother or me or you forever. You knew it better than me. Why don't you ever listen to anybody once you make up your stubborn mind. Once your pride orders you what to do. All that fine, mean pride, Daddy. All the mean years they put Rakhim away.

Why did you have to act like you know everything about judges, courts, law, just cause you're black and the cops tossed your belligerent ass in jail overnight a couple of times.

No, Daddy. Big Jim didn't try to touch me.

Latreesha, Big Jim, my father, the Tills gone. Too late now. I'm still hurting and angry anyway. Rakhim was only three or four years old the summer of 1955. How old will he be when they finally let him come home. *Mercy,* parole boards call it. Mercy to release him after a lifetime in prison. I'm afraid the board will wait until the tumor in his neck big as an orange. How many months out before the tumor strangles him.

Where are you, Latreesha. I've never forgotten you. How could I. Your devilish eyes. Silky smooth skin light and bright as my mother's. I'll never forget tugging down the elastic waistband of your madras Bermuda shorts. Slowly, slowly. Afraid to go too fast. Afraid if I take too long *poof,* you'll be gone. Sofa bed empty. Me left alone with Grandma's snores bumpty-bump-bumptedy stumbling down the stairs.

You were the first, Latreesha. I'd never seen a real girl up close that way before. Only white women in magazines in Henderson's. Of course, I haven't forgotten. Remember inch by inch. You raised your hips, kicked your legs to help me get you naked. I didn't want to miss anything. Scared I'd do it wrong. Could hear my heart thump. Yours. Could you hear mine. Did you feel my heat, my heart like I felt yours. You touched me. Sweet, gentle touches. You sucked in your breath then slowly let it go. Breath, like words whispered in my ear. Your touches were words, too.

Where have you been all this time. All these years and years since. First love. Buster of my thirteen- or fourteen-year-old boy's cherry that Emmett Till summer I thought I'd become a man then quickly became a boy again. Then a dead boy.

I undressed you slow motion and rushed into you. Patience gone. Cool fled. I couldn't stop. You twisted. Jerked away. We left a tiny puddle on my grandmother's sofa.

Trying to go slow, but everything was over fast. Telltale scent afterwards. Would your father smell it when he got home from work. I hadn't been close to the ocean yet, so had no memories of it to help me place the odor. I thought Vicks VapoRub, deli pickles floating in brine.

Once back in our clothes we gave the sofa's plastic cover a good scrub with a dishrag and paper towels from your father's neater than a pin kitchen where he fixed and ate his solitary meals before you arrived. No female company allowed in my church lady grandmother's house until you came along that summer to help out your father and escape bad Harlem streets, bad Harlem boys. I scrubbed and scrubbed. Worried your father or my busybody grandmother would see a stain and tattle to my mother. Poor Grandma, always sickly after Eugene didn't come home after the war. So blind if a bullfrog squatting on the sofa she wouldn't see it unless it croaked. What did we do with the incriminating evidence, those wads of crumpled paper towel, guilty dishcloth. Did we throw away the dishrag with the paper. I don't remember, but I do recall every inch by inch of you. How fine you were. How good it felt to lie next to you Latreesha. I wanted everybody in the world to know, but back then I couldn't tell a soul. Certainly not my father, most certainly not my mother. Not my loudmouth, teasing crew or fat, grinning Jim Saunders either. Big Jim the busybody, gossipy, rhino-sized man who paid cash for a brand-new three-tone Merc and claimed he knew you, spoke with you, but whether he did, Latreesha, or not, he didn't need to hear every little detail of a fourteen-year-old boy and thirteen-year-old girl kissing, hugging, getting it on in the dark.

I was the one who needed dark. You didn't ask me to turn off the lamp beside the sofa, did you. I'm the one said, *Better not unfold the sofa.* I'm the one killed the light, even though I yearned to see you top to toes. Toes painted the same fast pink as your fingernails. I turned off the lamp because I didn't want you to see too much of me. My scrawny chest, bony arms, big feet with no socks in stinky sneakers, raggedy, gray drawers under my hoop shorts.

You knew a lot more about boys than I knew about girls. Harlem wise about everything. Your tight jeans rode low on your hips like I'd seen only white boys in movies wear them. You stopped me when I tried to remove your T-shirt. *Huh-uh. No, no, mister. Leave it be. Saving my titties for my husband.* Punched my shoulder with the heel of your hand as you twisted out from under me. *You crazy, boy. No rubber. No. No. No. Don't you know no better.*

You scared me, Latreesha. I thought I had hurt you. Or maybe you had changed your mind. Truth is, I didn't think. I was gone. So full of myself I exploded. Too late then to do anything but try and figure out what happened while I'd been away.

Before we tidied up the mess, while we were still side by side, half-naked in the dark on Grandma's plastic-wrapped sofa, neither of us said a word. I thought maybe you were upset. Then you sat up quickly, scrambled over me like enough of this foolishness and you wanted to put on your clothes. You scooted, bumped me out of your way as you got up, and I had to drop my hand to the floor to keep from rolling off the edge. Next thing I know, you lean down, give my penis a kiss, a quick peck more like a touch than a kiss but it made my whole body shiver. I hoped you missed the sticky spot and wondered if I should kiss you down where you kissed me. Wondered if kissing your lips after they touched my private part would be like kissing it myself.

You snuggled down with me again after you'd used the bathroom, shut up my dumb questions, my worries with your tongue searching for mine inside my mouth. All those dumb questions, and here's another for you. Or a couple, I guess. On this first visit after so many years, is it strange for me to ask, Latreesha, strange for me to think you might know the answer. Did Emmett Till ever get a chance to make love.

II

THE FILE

The policy of the War department is not to intermingle colored and white enlisted personnel in the same regimental organizations. This policy has proven satisfactory over a long period of years, and to make changes now would produce situations destructive to morale and detrimental to the preparation for national defense. It is the opinion of the War Department that no experiments should be tried with the organizational set up of these units at this crucial time.

(DRAFT OF U.S. MILITARY'S PLAN OF INTEGRATION, SENT TO PRESIDENT FRANKLIN D. ROOSEVELT AND SIGNED BY HIM INTO LAW)

All men are cautioned to treat [colored soldiers] with respect but not to cultivate friendship with them.

Under this printed poster, a handwritten note: *For the best interest of everyone, stay completely away from them.*

(POSTED ON BARRACKS DOOR, FORT HOOD, TEXAS)

From an initial wave of tens of thousands of colored men who volunteered for military duty at the outset of World War II, only a few were inducted immediately into the armed services. Over three hundred thousand colored volunteers drifted in limbo as late as February 1943 while the War Department debated if it wanted them, if colored troops were worth the trouble, and what to do with them if they became armed forces personnel. Louis Till was an exception, a lucky one snapped up in 1942 for active duty as soon as he enlisted.

From *Smithsonian* magazine's April 2011 issue commemorating the 150th anniversary of the Civil War's first shot, I learned that slaves had manned the oars of a launch bearing representatives of the newly created Confederacy on a mission to offer Federal troops safe passage from Fort Sumter, a fort the Federals occupied illegally according to the delegation in the launch, since the fort in Charleston, South Carolina's harbor and South Carolina had declared itself part of a new, sovereign nation. The rambunctious, rebellious south unable to avert war or start war without strong-backed Negroes to propel its delegates across Charleston harbor, delegates bearing an ultimatum for Fort Sumter's commanding officer.

Tell your boss, Mr. Lincoln, he best leave us and our Negroes be. Everything will be just fine and dandy if you yankees go back where you belong and we'll stay down here where we belong and youall can do what you please with your Negroes and we'll do as we please with ours.

April 1861. The South Carolina sky is the color of a scowl, color of a howl. I cross between shore and island, the boat I'm in plying water salty as a wound. Deep silence broken only by bright feathers of water drip-dripping from the tips of oars when they are lifted and we glide with the current, drifting so we don't approach too swiftly, too presumptuously the gun ports staring down on us from Fort Sumter's stone ramparts. Six rowing, four riding, which makes ten in the launch. Plus me. Stop. Ten *What.* Not ten southern gentlemen. Not ten slaves. Ten constituted by units of *what.* A question not even a bloody, bloody civil war resolves. Ten a muddling of kinds. Muddling of races. Ten a fiction. Like my presence in the boat. So let's just say four delegates on a dire mission ride their property, and six pieces of property ride the delegates from Charleston harbor to Fort Sumter aboard a launch flying a white flag.

Louis Till pulls hard on his oar, strokes slightly out of sync with the other rowers. Same ole, lost-in-space, pay no attention to nobody or nothing Till, if you listen to Peabo tell it. Peabo sitting on a cross-plank two planks behind Louis Till's plank, out of Louis Till's sight, but Till doesn't need to see him to know fat lip, mutter-mouth Peabo is muttering. Peabo's always busy muttering, googling his one good eye to catch anybody who listens to what he mutters, somebody to nod amen. Light hangs lazy as silk above the stillish water. Crimson blush fades from the horizon and Till recolors it red as Mary's barrel-ass behind snuggled in a red silk dress yesterday morning sashshaying at sunup from the Big House back to the quarters.

Louis Till likes music while he works. The others singing, him listening makes work go faster. But ain't nobody ask him what he like. Boat quiet as a grave waiting for a body to be rolled in. After they damn niggers and shoo niggers out the way who ain't in the way, clumsy boots rocking the boat and stepping on niggers' bare toes. After they shove and damn niggers some more, same niggers spozed to catch them, pick them up if they fall in the boat or fall in the water. After all this these white men real quiet.

Some business got them tongue-tied, tight-lipped this morning. White faces whiter, even the white face ruddy as a rutabaga and the white face yam colored. Not a word from the white men who stare at niggers working the oars like the niggers carrying them to market to sell.

Most the time crackers don't give a fuck what they say in front of niggers. Your average nigger dumb as a boll weevil what they think. But ole boll weevil hear what he hear and do what he got to do. White people trying they best every day to kill boll weevil but Mr. Weevil still going strong. Till wouldn't say this shit out loud to Peabo or Fred McMurray. More like grin it, smirk it, cough it in the middle of somebody saying something else. Till good at signifying. Wrinkle up his nose. Wink. Wag his big head *huh-uh* while his mouth says yes. Till's long eyelashes droop like he's nodding off, then one eye pop wide open. Peep up at Peabo like it's a whole nother world inside his head nobody but him and Peabo can see.

Louis Till turns up his nose. Lets everybody know he's trying not to smell the stink of stale meat inside a velvet-trimmed, gold-buttoned coat stretched tight as a sail full of wind across the wide back of the man in front of him. White man stiff as a board trying not to wobble as the boat pitches and wobbles. Till wonders do cows stink to cows. Pigs stink to pigs. Do pigs stink to cows. Cows to pigs. Stink of cow or pig say good eating to a wolf. If it's your kind you don't eat, ain't no point sniffing round it. Forget about it. Row. Row this boat of white men worried stinking quiet about something.

I sit invisible in the launch. We pitch more with more open water under us. I'm next to a delegate from Georgia, our cross-plank between Peabo's and Till's. I'm smiling at the naked joke of the South's precarious ride on the shoulders of slave power. Not exactly news to me, of course, but until I came across the *Smithsonian* article I'd never entered this moment, savored this crystal-clear image, this epiphany: slaves rowing their masters to perdition. Never shared a boat with Louis Till and his crew, with solemn emissaries from the Confederacy who want to believe they're slick and tough enough to divide a country and put a goodly portion of it in their pockets and think nobody in Washington will holler. *Stop thief.*

A familiar figure posed tall in the launch's prow. Looks like the noble silhouette of George Washington crossing the Delaware. But no, excuse me, it's John Brown: *I am now quite certain that the crimes of this guilty land will never be purged away, but with blood.*

June 27, 1944, near the Italian town of Civitavecchia, all hell broke loose. At approximately ten thirty that evening an air-raid alert sounded and searchlights leaped into the black sky. A thunderous barrage of forty-millimeter and ninety-millimeter antiaircraft cannons boomed. During the next hour and a half, while salvos of artillery continued to flash and rumble and searchlights comb the darkness and sirens wail in response to the false alarm of an enemy raid, two Italian women are allegedly raped, another woman shot in the belly and killed. American soldiers encamped in the vicinity would be accused of the crimes, and two colored privates, Louis (NMI) Till and Fred A. McMurray, were hanged, July 2, 1945, after a court-martial conducted by army officers found them guilty of the Civitavecchia rapes and murder.

* * *

Everybody's dead and dirty, dirty and dead inside the copy of the record of trial of *United States v. Louis Till (CMZ288642)* arriving finally in the mail from the United States Court of Criminal Appeals, Arlington, Virginia, the file I have subsequently read and reread, mining it for facts, for whatever the substance might be that connects fact to fact, the sea upon which facts float, the sea that drowns facts.

If I didn't already know what to expect, the color of the file's cover warns me that its contents, on over two hundred 8½ x 14 inch, white-bordered pages of the same unsettling hue as the cover, will not be nice. The color of the photocopied pages is unnameable. Presumably, the original pages were entirely white once, white as only their edges are white today. White like a hopelessly soiled pillowcase might have been white once upon a time. The unpleasant color of the pages a history of what's been done to the file, and I can't help feeling a bit guilty and ashamed. Pages the color of my dried sweat and dirt and spit and snot. Color of my naked sleep, of where I sleep, who I sleep with, where sleep takes me and what my body leaves behind. I feel sorry for innocent pillowcases and for these pages of the Till file stained to the color of bandages wrapped around a mummy sealed thousands of years inside a dark, airless pyramid. The wrappings and dead skin indistinguishable. A dead, ugly color is what I see, and most everybody within the file probably dead, too, in the half century plus since daylight last touched it. Then suddenly the document exhumed, each page duplicated by the flashbulb glare of a copy machine. Old, dirty secrets exposed to anyone who requests a transcript. The dead startled awake from uneasy sleep. Sleep the color of the file's pages.

After an initial tingle of anticipation as I leafed through it, I couldn't bring myself to begin reading. Fear detoured me, fear and suspicion. Fear that too much is at stake. Or nothing at all. Suspicion of my motives. Fear of failure. So I delay, equivocate, postpone. Ancient habits, just in case I might not get what I want. Just in case I do. Why hurry. Disappointment will settle in soon enough. What would I be missing, after all, if the file sat an hour, a day, a year. If I never read a single word.

Till file arrives. I had imagined many times how I'd feel with the file finally in my hands. None of my imaginings came close to what actually transpired. After I opened the envelope and peeked at the contents, I turn my back on the file. Go to another room. Plop down in a comfortable leather chair. A lot or a little time elapses before I hear a voice say, *you have a funny name for a black dude.* A familiar voice from a particular time and place, but I couldn't recall when, where, who said those words to me. I drift off again. Found myself thinking about turkey. Thanksgiving turkey with all the trimmings. I watch my sister heap a plate with mashed potatoes, candied yams, string beans, stuffing, greens with fatty morsels of ham hock, jellied cranberries, a thick slice of breast, chunks of dark meat sprinkled with giblet gravy which she pours also into a crater of mashed potatoes and copiously over a mound of corn-bread stuffing, then she crosses the roomful of family, everybody too busy eating to do much talking. They grin at each other, quietly laugh at jokes nobody needs to tell out loud. Only a few real old folks are left who'd watched over me when I was a boy. Many new, fresh faces of kids. Nephews and nieces. Cousins' kids, kids of kids, too many to keep track of names. Their foreign sounding, new age, space age, born yesterday, hip-hop names I try to keep straight in my mind but can't. Sis remembers them all, nodding with the music of each one as she speaks it, passing by with that brimming plate and her brimming smile prettier, more stately and elegant, more beaming, more and more like our mother as Sis ages. My little sister has grandkids of her own. Sis like Mom serves generations of family growing up, growing old, growing away. Sis well on her way to becoming the center, the glue now that Mom's too old and infirm to be perpetually on duty. My sister grips the loaded platter in two hands like a steering wheel, maneuvers it around bodies, chairs, heavy old pieces of scarred, polished, mahogany-colored furniture crowding a room way too small for all the people in it if all the people here had not gathered in this smallish room or other small rooms with big furniture in small houses for the express purpose of crowding into one another's way, glorying in the overabundance of flesh, of food, of noise they could generate together, up close, in the close quarters of bumping, of booming laughter, of call and response. When someone gets a good tale going, everybody listens or half listens or overhears, amens, yes, no, *maybe, no way, you lie like a rug.*

Sometimes I steal a precious momentary escape from family packed in the small room. Take a break to hear myself chew, think my own thoughts above the din. Absolutely alone for a necessary minute, before I sneak in a little private, half-whispered conference with somebody near my age I've not seen since last year's gathering, and we remember together old secrets we share and won't talk very much about now, probably never. But so good to see that other person still around in the flesh, still keeping alive secrets there's no possibility anyone else on earth can ever share.

This small room is more than big enough for everybody in the entire Pittsburgh family to squeeze in, squeeze out, if and when they choose. Everybody together, jammed up close for a lifetime, a minute in the room through which Sis guides a plate, deftly negotiating familiar traffic till she sets it down on the little folding stand beside Mom in her wheelchair. When Sis got up to fix her a plate, Mom said, Thank you, baby. Aren't you a sweet daughter to your old, decrepit mother, and said, Just a little something, Sis, she said, Not much appetite anymore, but Sis knows as well as I know that Mom will lick the platter clean like she taught her children they always must do, and then she'll say yes to just a smidgen of blueberry cobbler or a corner of her last remaining sister Aunt Geraldine's butter pound cake or maybe just a tiny taste of both, Thank you, honey.

The roomful of family is real enough to break my heart. Then the room dissolves. Gone. Just like daily specials listed on a blackboard at a restaurant across a cobbled terrace in an Italian city where I'm staying. Old specials wiped away. No turkey today. A swipe of wet rag and that ancient family dinner erased. A piece of chalk in the waiter's hand poised to post today's menu quick as the board dries.

Mom gone. Small room empty. Smaller and smaller. Speck in my eye. Sis hobbling around on a cane now after her hip operation. How many nieces with babies before they finish high school, how many nephews or nephews' sons on the streets dealing drugs or slammed up in the joint. Or dead in an alley. Stop.

Been there, done that. Don't start the count. The goddamn countdown. Lurid statistics a mantra of white noise. Nobody hears the appalling, shameful numbers anymore anyway. How many dead. How many trapped and dying. On principle I refuse to repeat the daunting statistics or say the word *genocide*. Suspicious of people who do and do nothing. The family's young ones, whose names I've never truly learned, maimed already. The old ones too tough and stubborn to die, but can't remember their own names. Silent in beds, wheelchairs, staring the whole damn day out windows of nursing homes.

A giant, golden, roasted Thanksgiving bird, pan juice crackling when I surreptitiously open the oven and peek in. Gleaming rivulets sweat down the turkey's sides. Deep-breasted, plump thighs, splayed legs skewered together at the ankles. Nubs where feet used to be. Daydreaming a big bird. Open my eyes and see big bones picked clean. I remember the Till file sits on the desk where I left it. Waits patiently as if it had always been there. As if it had never been lost. Never disappeared.

I had expected more drama. More than a faint hiss, a whiff of staleness when I slit open the large yellow envelope and extracted the Till file. A long wait for its arrival. I'd been impatient, then anxious, finally convinced it wasn't coming. There's a certain comfort in waiting. Waiting in line, waiting for a subway. Waiting for freedom. For old age, death. Waiting lets you off the hook. You just wait. Waiting becomes a habit. Part reprieve, part hiding place. Waiting for the clock's next tick. Waiting for something even when you're sure it will never occur. Waiting concedes that what happens next is beyond your control. So wait. Wait and see. Or not see.

After my first few readings of the file, I was as suspicious of the order of pages as I'd been of their color. The pages of the Louis Till file are not numbered consecutively. Nor arranged chronologically, except perhaps by a confusing rule, broken often, a rule like Frantz Fanon's that *first is last and last first.* The confusion may be terminal. Initial sections of the file contain events whose date (1955) make them closest to the reader's present time, and since they stand at the front of the file, a reader begins at the end of the story the file narrates and reads towards its beginning, but events from the beginning of the file's time sequence (1944) also appear in early sections so a reader begins at the story's start and reads towards its end in this collection of reports, judicial reviews, letters, telegrams, death certificates, court orders, invoices, legal opinions, expense vouchers, postscripts, newspaper articles, et cetera attached to the transcript of the joint court-martial of Louis Till and Fred McMurray.

To impose a bit of order on the unwieldy contents I penciled numbers on the file's pages. Most bore typed numbers designating their place within a section, but no running count connected the sections. The court-martial transcript, for instance, by far the longest consecutively numbered segment, comes near the file's end, but it is numbered 1–96. After the court-martial section, I stopped my numbering project because only a few pages followed its last page. Stopped also because by then I understood my numbers simply reaffirmed, without challenging or clarifying, the order of the file's contents when it arrived in my mailbox.

The Till file's pages are bound by a strip of metal that functions like a giant, reusable staple passing through two holes punched in the top of every sheet. Staple's grooved ends slide together and lock. A snake devouring itself. Who determined the sequence into which the pages had been bound. Perhaps the copy I received retained the order in which pages had originally been filed. Or had a clerk taken the file's first page, duplicated it, placed it face-up, then stacked other pages face-up as they emerged from the copier, thus exactly reversing the original order. But in the government's Virginia archive the process would be high-tech not manual, wouldn't it. Feed an original into the mouth of a machine. Punch buttons. Presto. Original scanned, digitized, replicated, paginated, stapled, bound et cetera. Choice of size and color.

Determining whether or not a machine had assembled the file wouldn't answer questions I needed answered. Had someone rigged the file to be read in a particular fashion. Who. When. Why. Were the trial transcript and its accompanying documents organized sixty years ago or just yesterday in response to my Freedom of Information (FOI) request. Had anyone alive or dead ever bothered to read, let alone attempt to manipulate, the Till file pages. Was the person (yesterday or six decades previously) who unearthed, organized, and dispatched the file, following orders. What orders. Whose orders. Like Emmett Till in the box bringing him home to Chicago from Mississippi, Louis Till's story in the file is damaged almost beyond recognition. Lost and found and lost.

* * *

A perfunctory note on a half sheet of U.S. Army letterhead stationery paper-clipped to the file's cover page identifies the name and number of the document and informs the recipient no fee is owed since the number of pages required to fulfill the FOI petition falls within the automatic waiver threshold and supplied to U.S. citizens by the government free of charge. This note signed by a woman whose name I tell myself each time I see it I should write down in my notebook for safekeeping. To thank. To pester for more. To hold responsible. To flirt. To forget.

On the cover a command printed in huge black letters is formatted like a poem:

THIS FILE TO BE
RETURNED
TO
J.A.G.O.
COURT-MARTIAL RECORDS
ROOM 3A 346 PENTAGON BUILDING

At the top of the cover a request is printed in small, underlined *capital* letters, PLEASE DO NOT WRITE ON THIS BACKER. This admonition had been ignored by numerous people who penciled numbers and dates here and there, many dark slashes censoring whatever's beneath them. Slanting across the left middle of the cover a dotted line bears a handwritten date, *14 October 1955,* followed by initials *RK,* then a scribbled surname difficult to decipher, and finally the signer's rank. Near the cover's bottom edge a serial number, *288642.* Just above it a smudge that almost but not quite hides the word *CONFIDENTIAL.*

CONFIDENTIAL stamped in large letters on the top and bottom of the file's second page. Lines drawn through *confidential* again. This second page is stamped, *CLASSIFICATION CANCELLED BY AUTHORITY OF TJAG,* and after the stamp comes a handwritten signature authorizing the cancellation. Date, name and rank of signer more legible this time than the scrawl on the dotted line slanting across the file's cover.

Each time the October 14 date appeared, I wondered if I had discovered a smoking gun. Doesn't a conspiracy to violate Private Louis Till's right to privacy originate there, on that day in October 1955, just after the Sumner trial when Till's confidential military service record is declassified and the way cleared for the file's contents to be leaked to the press. Just in time to sabotage any likelihood a Mississippi grand jury might convene in November and decide to try Milam and Bryant on kidnapping charges.

If I had been asleep at the switch and missed the telltale October date, it reappears two pages later on a memorandum addressed to the office of the judge advocate general (JAG). The cover page of the long memo names its subject as *Louis Till, formerly Pvt. 36392273,* and lists as its contents a series of enclosures, some of which are included, some not in my copy of the file. At the bottom of the memo a circular official seal certifies the memo's date of dispatch, *14 Oct 1955,* and above it, typed this time, the name of *Ralph K. Johnson, Colonel, JAG chief, Military Justice Division,* the officer who facilitated the release of classified documents. In response to some unnamed but very powerful person's request, rules had been broken and the Louis Till File, buried ten years in an archive, had been disinterred, disturbed, the remains shipped by the judge advocate general's office to the press and to lawyers defending Emmett Till's killers.

But the October 14, 1955, date is not necessarily smoke curling from a guilty gun barrel. If Emmett Till's murderers committed no crime, then no conspiracy to cover up a crime exists. What would be accomplished if I were to shout the October date from the rooftops of New York City or Money, Mississippi. A redneck senator's vicious meddling (later, he proudly admitted his role in an interview), and an accommodating army officer's betrayal of a fellow soldier's privacy were minor trespasses, once I began to grasp the gravity of wrongdoing recorded in the Till file.

I've read the Louis Till file cover to cover many times now. I'm all too familiar with its frustrating discontinuities, helter-skelter chronology, bits and pieces of handwritten military dispatches and typed correspondence tossed in with no apparent rhyme or reason, one section interrupted or repeated by another, pages missing, pages playing hide-and-seek. The document I received from the government archives in Virginia is a hodgepodge of this and that, making sense sometimes, sometimes not. Like history. History in general or any individual life history in particular. Mine, for example. Yours. Ours. History a vanished city, erased by war or flood or fire or earthquake. Or many cities collapsed one atop another over the centuries, buried under miles and miles of sand.

However, each time I reach the end of the file—Louis Till and Fred McMurray hanged, Junior Thomas exonerated—the ironies are too bitter. Too final. I'm diminished by what I've learned.

Common sense says step back, take a deep breath, a long view. But I can't. Any peace of mind I try to cobble together is mocked by power. Power that controls the record. Displays and deploys the record. Power that smirks at me. Power putting words in Louis Till's mouth. Power imprisoning, executing colored soldiers, young colored men cut down war or no war. Power importantly clearing its throat, *Hrrrrhumph,* as it delivers the last word on Louis Till.

The literal last word on the last page of the Till file is *Confidential,* stamped at the bottom of a letter written in February 1945 by a Brigadier General Oxx to the commanding officer of the infamous MTOUSA (Mediterranean Theater of Operations, United States Army) Disciplinary Training Center. The letter releases Private James Thomas, Junior, from prison and transfers him, the snitch who doomed Till, from the company he served in with Till and McMurray to another company of the 379th. Someone drew lines through *Confidential,* but you can still see the word at the bottom of the file's final page. The job of some enlisted men, probably, to make sure *Confidential* was crossed out on all two hundred plus pages just as on the file's cover. Power transforming *Confidential* into a ghost word, dead and alive, invisible and present. An ironic word. A word meaning something and nothing. A word everywhere and nowhere in the file. Silenced and speaking like lynched Louis Till.

I close the last page and I'm certain again that nothing about the record is accidental. The Till file works the way any good, old-fashioned novel works. It may sprawl all over the known world, but by the final scene, the plot's resolved, accounts settled, order restored, characters receive their just deserts. Which means somebody's been telling a story. Somebody's been in control. Then the story's over. Ending the only way it could end, the way it was supposed to end from the first word, first page. The file irreversible. An unwavering witness. Story's finished, and I'm left out. Take it or leave it. Nowhere to hide.

I compel myself to go back to the beginning. Resist the ugly story. Resist the reality these stapled-together documents construct. Even if my resistance only confirms a reality damaged beyond repair.

And here's something else, just as unsettling as power's smirk, as the ugliness the discolored, disorderly pages embody. While I read the file, so much fear and busyness stirred up around Private Louis Till, it's easy to forget how young he was. Only a kid. Barely twenty-three years old minus two years, nine months stolen by war and prison. Till's only chance for a life, his only story, only portion over quickly. Pages read and reread, renumbered or not, will not change this truth. Truth of how soon Louis Till's life ends. A very young person cut down. Then his son Emmett, cut down at fourteen, gets nine years less of life than his father. Nothing I read or write will buy the Tills more time. Nothing stops the greedy, crazed old men who eat their children.

I'm wide awake. Grope for the phone on a night table beside the bed. Did its ringing wake me. Will it ring again. My hand overturns and recalls at the same instant a glassful of water I'd set beside the phone. Stillness and darkness amplified by the phone's abrupt silence when it stops ringing. A glass shattering sounded like a dozen glasses. Too late, but I warn my arm anyway. Be careful. Remember the water I set out to keep me company. Suddenly the air conditioner thuds on, shuddering in its metal casing. Where were you when I needed you, motherfucker. Then I remember I'm in another country. Nothing here speaks English. It's sultry Italian air bathing me in sweat. I need to pee. As I swing my legs over to what I hope is the safe side of the floor, a fist starts to bram on the door. Louder and louder. Then a voice from the other side. *Dat boy from Chicago in dere. You got the one did the talking in dere.*

One masked intruder carried a gun, the Till file informs me. After the men burst through the door, one of them lit a match. Match light was enough, victims claimed, to pick out a face's color under a hood in the pitch-black shack. Three intruders. Three of them, *three colored men . . . negroes . . . niggers,* swore the inhabitants of the raided Mari residence in Civitavecchia. Four of us raided, swore the accused in their testimony. This major discrepancy—were there three or four assailants—is never questioned by defense attorneys during the court martial of Louis Till and Fred McMurray.

The Mari *shack* or *barracks* or *shanty,* as it was variously identified in the file, consisted of two rooms, both opening onto a passageway or corridor that leads to the single entrance. The larger of the two small rooms was divided by a partition. Frieda Mari slept on one side of the partition, her parents, Ernetto Mari and Guila Persi, on the other. Benni Lucretzia and her daughter, Elena, refugees who'd just arrived in Civitavecchia from the bombed-out village of Allumiere, occupied a negligible space behind the Mari-Persi room. The cramped barracks (a crude diagram included in the file) afforded little or no privacy, depending on the sleeping area in which a bed was located.

Though no enemy planes transgressed the night skies above Civitavecchia on June 27, 1944, antiaircraft artillery rumbled and searchlights probed, frightening civilians, scrambling the American troops garrisoned at camps nearby. Frieda Mari, closely trailed by the girl Elena, had bolted from her bed to the shack's door, flung it open to escape falling walls or to see for herself what new terror war was delivering. She never got beyond the door. Masked men shooed her and Elena back inside the darkness. Colored men she was sure, she said, because the intruders lit matches. One of them was tall, she said. Dark-skinned, five foot, ten inches. Another shorter, light-skinned, five foot, six inches, and the third, the shortest one, a mulatto, whitest of the three. Later, while the shortest, whitest one is on top of her, Frieda Mari testifies she lifts the hoodlike mask off his face. The glimpse she steals leaves no doubt in her mind, she tells judges at the court-martial. Her attacker was a mulatto. Asked by a juror what color exactly she had seen in the darkness, Frieda Mari replies: *He wasn't very light. He was sort of a light dark or clear dark.* The juror (looking around the courtroom where Till and McMurray sit) goes on to ask: *Is there anyone in this room that would have the color of this person.* Frieda Mari answers. *There aren't any.*

No, all witnesses agree: Too dark to tell what color clothing the attackers wore. Yes, all witnesses agree: we could see the color of the invaders' skin.

In spite of darkness broken only by an occasional match or flashes from antiaircraft guns and searchlights penetrating the shack's flimsy walls, in the file the victims provide uncannily consistent and precise physical descriptions of the intruders. Three witnesses identify one man's height as five foot, ten inches, another man as five foot, six inches. At least that's what statements prepared by Criminal Investigation Division investigators assert. Maybe CID agents simply reported what they heard during interviews. Maybe not. The statements are in English. Presumably the victims spoke Italian, so the statements have been translated. Measurements expressed in inches and feet are conversions from centimeters and meters. Spoken words have been *reduced* (CID agents' term of art) to typed summaries. Translation. Conversion. Reduction. Each process transforms a witness's words. Each creates a step away, further and further away, from the words of live encounters between CID agents and witnesses. I grant the agents the benefit of the doubt. Assume they did their best to render accurately the words of people they interviewed, and still—translation, conversion, reduction produce at best problematic, at worst unreliable, corrupted representations of conversations.

Suppose the English versions of interviews in the file were translated into Italian, the inches and feet converted to metrics. Would Italian witnesses recognize their original statements in these retranslations. Would they proclaim *Sì*, yes, those are my words.

My copy of the Till file begins with about thirty pages of miscellaneous correspondence, including notices certifying that Privates Louis (NMI) Till and Fred A. McMurray had been charged, tried, executed, and a newspaper clipping dated October 15, 1955, reporting that Louis Till had been hanged in 1945 for rapes and murder he committed in Italy. Then comes a long, detailed narrative, composed after the McMurray, Till court-martial, by an army board of review that describes the crimes of June 27–28 in Civitavecchia, Italy. Death certificates of Till and McMurray follow. Next comes the initial report of alleged Civitavecchia crimes compiled by Agents Herlihy and Rousseau of Criminal Investigation Division, Rome Allied Area Command (CID/RAAC #41) filed August 7, 1944. After snippets of administrative paperwork, two more postcourt-martial narratives of the crimes appear, both written like the initial narrative, by army officers whose job was to determine whether or not justice had been served. All three review board narratives tell the same story. Not surprising since they all depend solely, uncritically on information contained in the original investigative report (CID/RAAC #41) and testimony recorded in the court-martial transcript. Three repetitions of more or less the same story asserting violent details of who did what to whom have a chilling effect. Why would anyone reading the tale today challenge its impartiality.

No doubt about it. Some brutal, ugly shit went down in Civitavecchia. No counternarratives contest the accuracy, the veracity of what review boards report. Guilt of Till and McMurray a foregone conclusion when the court-martial transcript appears at the end of the Till file. Pretrial publicity with a vengeance. The court-martial transcript doesn't serve the reader as an opportunity for unbiased weighing of evidence. A guilty verdict arrives as a kind of I-told-you-so. A tail positioned in the file to wag the dog. From one review board text to the next, alleged facts pick up speed and weight, become an irresistible avalanche.

Review board writers adopt the omniscient voice of certain kinds of fiction (and nonfiction) that seem to grant readers the privilege of being detached, objective observers of the action. As if a video cam hovers above scenes and characters, an objective eye and ear reporting truth and only the truth. It's a convincing account unless a reader understands the scenarios presented by the words of review boards are not eyewitness reports of unbiased spectators present during the action, but *reductions of reductions.*

Testimony in the Till file may seem to come from many voices, but all voices are mediated by CID/RAAC agents. These agents, fellow officers of court-martial judges, gather evidence, take statements from witnesses and defendants, submit their finding to the prosecution (and sometimes to the defense). Conditions pertaining during the original CID interviews/interrogations—hour of night or day, duration, methods and incentives employed to extract information, who was present during questioning—remain unknown unless the agent preparing the reduction chooses to include such factors. This system provides agents ample, perhaps irresistible, opportunities for abuse.

Limited only by conscience and ingenuity, agents can manipulate, freelance, bypass entirely words of a witness. But witness statements enter the record and are treated as if they are taped depositions, the exact words of witnesses. The only authentication required is a second signature beneath the signature of the officer who files the reduction. Routinely this signature is supplied by a fellow agent.

Witness statements in the file establish minute details—an intruder's exact height—and leave major issues unsettled—how many men raided the Mari residence, how many women were sexually assaulted. For army officers at court-martial or serving on review boards, the cumulative weight of victim statements establish, beyond a shadow of a doubt, Louis Till and Fred McMurray as perpetrators, even though each individual victim admits that darkness, hoods, masks, shock, confusion made it impossible to identify the men who attacked them. Seated across the court-martial chamber from Till and McMurray, no victim could identify or accuse either man. Including Ernetto Mari, Frieda Mari's father, who had claimed in a previous statement recorded by CID agents that he had seen the three colored intruders outdoors, in broad daylight, near the Cisterna, a waterpoint in Civitavecchia, the afternoon following the night they'd raided his home and knocked him unconscious: *I saw the three men—the same three—behind the house of a neighbor.*

I was not present so I can't claim to know what transpired in a specific interview or sequence of interviews, but no doubt CID officers determined which words formed the final shape and meaning of testimony presented at court-martial. Telltale signs of *reduction* are abundant in both structure and content of victim statements. In Agent Barnes's version of what Benni Lucretzia and Frieda Mari said to him in their second recorded interviews (October 28, 1944) the last words of both statements deliver a punch line to remind the reader each woman was pregnant when assaulted. Both statements repeat identical phrases and words. *Push* must be one of Captain Barnes's favorite words; it appears six times in the twelve lines of one woman's statement, seven times in the other woman's.

When a witness speaks to court-martial judges (or to a reader of the Till file), it's fair to ask whose words issue from the witness's mouth. Off-camera interrogations allow agents to plant information, coach, coax, censor, coerce. The original recorded statements of Lucretia and Mari are each less than two hundred words. At court-martial each woman's testimony expands to include all the classic elements necessary for conviction of capital rape—violence, coercion, duration of the act, depth of vaginal penetration, sightings of the offender's penis, assertion of the victim's resistance, the aggravating presence of deadly weapons.

The fact that Till, McMurray, and the other alleged perpetrators were colored, plus the fact that Till and McMurray were reported in the vicinity of Civitavecchia the night the crimes occurred, is enough to convince army officers the accused are guilty. No further burden of proof is demanded from the prosecution. Privates Till and McMurray are sentenced to death on the basis of being the wrong color in the wrong place at the wrong time. *Wrong color, wrong place, wrong time,* a mantra. A crime that over the course of our nation's history has transformed countless innocent people of color into guilty people. The remainder of the case against Till and McMurray consists of conflicting, ambiguous hearsay evidence that for some reason, defense lawyers, except for a few timid objections, allowed to stand. On one rare occasion when defense lawyers did challenge the prosecution's case (a defense contention that Fred McMurray's written statement naming Louis Till as the ringleader of the fatal raid should be excluded because it was obtained by grilling McMurray for at least ten consecutive hours), court-martial judges quickly overruled the objection.

CID agents began their investigation of Anna Zanchi's murder unaware that two Italian women had been assaulted near the Zanchi residence the same night Anna Zanchi had been shot. With no murder weapon recovered from the Zanchi shooting, no motive, no suspects, the investigation of the Zanchi homicide was floundering and probably would have languished indefinitely unless someone stepped forward to confess or accuse. However, once CID agents heard rumors of rape by colored men, rapes occurring the night of the Zanchi shooting, their murder investigation proceeded rapidly, on firm footing. Rape and color paved the way. Saved the day. All the investigating officers needed were colored suspects, and the segregated 379th, a battalion full, was handy. Even better, agents already had in custody a bunch of colored sugar thieves.

Rape victims could be persuaded, unlike dead Anna Zanchi, to confirm the color if not the individual faces of assailants. Energized by rape and color, the investigation bulldozed ahead, more mission than inquiry. Color and rape provided a motive. Explain and link crimes on the night of June 27 as a single, predictable outburst of the well-known lust and violence that seethes barely suppressed in the dark blood of colored soldiers. A drunken, murderous, spree. A riot of uncontrollable, atavistic impulses. Colored soldiers whom the army considered second-class citizens were suspects who possessed no rights investigators need respect. The logic of southern lynch law prevailed. All colored males are guilty of desiring to rape white women, so any colored soldier the agents hanged could not be innocent.

On December 3, 1944, Mrs. Joyce MB of Bonfire Close, Chard, Somerset, England, married and in her ninth month of pregnancy, left her home to walk to the cinema. She was followed by Corporal Robert L. Pearson and Private Cubia Jones, both colored, of Company A, 1698th Engineer Combat Battalion, United States Army. The men, strangers to Mrs. MB, she said, walked up behind her, grasped her wrists and despite her protests that she was married and pregnant, dragged her into Bonfire orchard and raped her.

The next day in a lineup at the U.S. camp, Pearson and Jones were identified by Mrs. MB as her assailants and arrested. At trial Mrs. Joyce MB testified that she begged the soldiers repeatedly *Don't do it*, but the men ignored her pleas. She said that during the rape, they attempted to calm and console her by saying they loved her.

Corporal Pearson, twenty-one years old, and Private Jones, twenty-four, despite their contention that Mrs. MB consented to have sex, and despite their claims of love, were both found guilty of rape and subsequently hanged at Shepton Mallet prison, March 17, 1945, part of a wave of executions—including the judicial asphyxiation of Privates Till and McMurray—that resulted from a directive issued by General Eisenhower, Supreme Commander of Allied Forces in Europe and later President of the United States of America, ordering expeditious resolution of all pending cases alleging capital crimes committed by U.S. service personnel against foreign nationals.

What if the crimes of June 27–28, 1944, in Civitavecchia were not exactly rape, the criminals not exactly colored. CID agents, determined to prove color and rape, chose not to ask those questions. None of the obvious trails leading away from rape and color are pursued. No witness statement establishes the well-known fact elaborated by GIs' comments in the Till file that the assaulted shacks were situated in a cluster of hovels frequented day and night by American troops of all colors shopping for women and wine. No victim statement records whether sex for money was offered, requested, expected or obtained the night in question. Apart from accusations by the accused of other accused, no witness claims to have seen the same individuals present at both the rape and murder scenes. Only the perpetrators' color (or alleged color) links the assaults in one household with murder in another.

The victims declare that fear, panic, shock, chaos couldn't diminish their ability to recognize skin color. The victims elaborate upon various shades of colored skin they could discriminate in spite of the stygian gloom. Statements that might impede the agents' rush to blame color and rape are adjusted. John Masi, an Italian citizen who spoke English and asserted that he could distinguish colored voices from white voices because he'd lived a dozen years in Brooklyn, New York, had sworn in an initial statement (June 30, 1944) recorded by CID agents only forty-eight hours after the Zanchi shooting, that one of the two masked men who had pounded on the Zanchi door demanding sex and wine was white: "The tall one did most of the talking. From his actions and manner of speech I am of the opinion that he was white." Masi said that he had argued with two hooded, armed men on the porch of the Zanchi house for several minutes before they ordered him back inside and bullets blasted through the door killing his girlfriend's mother (CID Report #41).

A second interview (October 27, 1944) is arranged and Masi, by then an employee of the United States Military, reverses himself: "The American soldiers I talked to and who fired their pistols at the door of the casa of the Zanchi family, were colored Americans." In this second version of events, the version he repeated in his testimony at court-martial, not only has Masi become certain that he recognized a colored man's colored voice, he swears in effect that while lying on the floor he could see through a closed door the color of the man outside who fired fatal shots through it.

How many .45s were manufactured for the U.S. military during World War II—Louis Till allegedly stole a .45 automatic from a sailor on the night of June 27 and used it to kill Anna Zanchi—J. W. Milam's service .45 killed Louis Till's son—live by the .45, your son dies by the .45—justice or coincidence or irony—or none of the above—J. W. Milam was an MP—did he serve in Italy—did Milam bust colored soldiers from Till's battalion—could Louis Till and Milam have crossed paths during the war—did the same .45 kill Anna Zanchi and Emmett Till—what was the guilty .45's serial number—the weapon in the Zanchi shooting was identified as a .45 by shell casings on the ground at the crime scene, by holes in the Zanchi door, a big hole in the stomach of the dead woman—a .45 was never recovered by investigators—no victim identified Louis Till as the intruder who shot Zanchi—did the mysterious English guy Chappie eventually identified by CID agents as Private Frank Emmanuel, 903787, 6th Battalion, Gordon Highlanders, C Company, CMF (Canadian Military Forces), borrow a .45 from Till the night of June 27—was the .45 in the Canadian/Englishman's possession a month later when he was shot and killed by an Italian civilian at Maenza, near Terracina, Italy, during a holdup attempt—who was robbing whom—did J. W. Milam sneak his army sidearm back to the States or buy a different .45 after he returned home—who sold Milam a .45 in Mississippi—a .45 Milam liked to show off to his sharecroppers, people say—a war souvenir he shoved into Emmett Till's ear to scare him, smashed across Till's skull when Emmett didn't seem scared enough, pulled the trigger and blew out the boy's brains when scaring wasn't good enough—was the English-sounding guy a colored gay guy hanging around AWOL in a U.S. Army colored barracks with Louis Till, Fred McMurray and Junior

Thomas—was this Chappie, as he was known, fucking Junior Thomas on the sly—did Thomas with his gay lover, the foreign soldier, hustle and rob gay sailors—is that how the Zanchi murder weapon was obtained—after the Mari barracks attack, did Chappie and Thomas, not Till and McMurray, raid the Zanchi shack—did Chappie or Thomas shoot a .45 through the closed door—the plot thickens.

What if the person who prepared the Till file to be read by others had decided not only that Louis Till's voice must be heard, but that it must be heard first. What if a reader of the file could enter its pages without being assaulted by the same unforgiving tale repeated by three review boards. What if the voices of Till's wife, Mamie Till, or Till's son, Emmett, or a buddy of Louis Till from the 379th Port Battalion, a colored GI not on trial for murder, were included in the file. What if the file included the hurry-up memo from General Eisenhower ordering expeditious completion of all capital court-martials in Europe. Or included statistics documenting the stunningly disproportionate number of colored soldiers accused, convicted, and executed for rape. Or included the fact that systematic discrimination limited the number of colored soldiers in the officer corps and thus very few were available to staff court-martials and review boards. Voices recorded in the file have been orchestrated to engage in a conversation solely among themselves, a conversation condemning Till by excluding his voice, a conversation not acknowledging, let alone pondering the meaning of Till's silence.

Louis Till an orphan in his file, just as he'd started life as an orphan in New Madrid, Missouri. Guilty of being nobody long before a court-martial tries and convicts him, delivers his death sentence. He is born a colored orphan, and he dies one. A nobody. No voice, no room for Till inside or outside the file's pages. Till doomed by cracks within cracks within the legal system. Cracks in the yellow-gray transcript. The file's stuttering, helter-skelter chronology avoids and silences Till, a file already contaminated, problematic once Till's right of confidentiality scratched off the cover ten years after the document was legally sealed in 1945.

Everybody in the Till file lies. It's easy to recognize situations that compel lies. Benni Lucretzia's desperate concern to protect her daughter Elena's honor and marriageability; Fred McMurray's last-ditch attempt to keep his neck out of a noose. Junior Thomas blames others to exonerate himself; CID agents' desire to construct an open-and-shut case to meet a superior officer's demand for swift justice. If a reward is enticing enough, does the temptation to lie become irresistible. Do extreme circumstances mitigate lies. Do all questions deserve true answers—*is that boy from Chicago in there—are you hiding Jews in your cellar—Tutsis in your attic.* It's not easy for a reader of the file to figure out if a false story is being told because the teller believes it's true. Or to figure out if a story is suppressed because the person not telling it believes it's false. When is silence a lie. Can silence protect truth from the contamination of lies. It's exceedingly difficult to figure the *how* and *why* of lies. Difficult to accept that a tangle of self-interested deceptions is as close to truth as anybody ever gets.

Where does one lie end and another lie start. Each party has heavily invested in his or her portion of lies. In the file, until a court-martial passes judgment and decides which version of events wins, all lies are equal. All lies except colored lies. Colored lies (or truth, or fiction) are invalid unless they substantiate white lies. Lying is a weapon nobody in the Till file can afford to surrender. The collective enterprise of lying creates a sort of stock market. A Ponzi scheme. A market trading solely in worthless commodities. The only value and appeal of the stocks is that they postpone temporarily a reckoning of their worthlessness. They can be bought and sold and profit accrued as long as someone listens to the lie or believes the lie or pretends to believe the lie. Ensconced in a make-believe kingdom like Prospero's enchanted island in *The Tempest,* stocks are granted substance, habitation, names. Nobody invested in this chimerical market wants it to crash because their profitable lies will come tumbling down with the rest. The players wheel and deal as if the web of lies will never unravel, never unwind or wind up or wind down or do whatever lies do, whatever stocks do, lives do, fictions do, when the game's over. Like everybody else I'm invested in my own little portfolio of lies, set aside for rainy days. My lies true as any others till Prospero snaps his magic wand.

Will a moment finally emerge in which a collection of lies offers access to truth. More truth, anyway, than a single individual—liar or honest person—is capable of reconstructing. Which lies. Whose lies. The file writes fiction. To mimic reality, the Till file writes fiction.

Cut through the knotted lies. Cut to the chase. *Lights. Action. Camera.* As in blockbuster movies and novels. *Bam. Bloom.*

Boom. Booming guns snatch half-naked Frieda Mari from sleep, drive her to the door of a shack in Civitavecchia, a door she flings open to escape the terror of ceilings and walls crashing down.

What Benni Lucretzia sees first from her bed when cannon fire shakes the flimsy wooden shack is a blur of white nightgown, then her daughter, Elena, running towards the door, a little ghost trailing the big ghost of Frieda Mari's nightdress. Then Frieda and Elena are flying back through the shack, men chasing them who must have piled through the door when Frieda unlatched it.

Another world bursts into the dark barracks. Men have fallen from the sky, rushed through the open door. Screams. Shouts. A hand grips Benni Lucretzia's arm. Grunted words she doesn't understand. The room's full of huge, dark wings battering the air. A herd of panicked sheep, wolves in pursuit, wolves growling, barking, teeth snapping. The snarl of wolf language.

She's grabbed, shoved back down on her bed. Door slams. A match flickers. Shadows lift, lurch, spin. Black masks. White eyes gleam through eyeholes. A blinding flash snuffs the match, restores utter dark. Benni Lucretzia screams, Where is Elena. Where is my girl. Run, Elena. Run and hide. A heavy hand over Benni Lucretzia's mouth, another hand inside her nightgown. Gown rips when she wrenches away. She struggles to stay upright, her back wedged against the wall. Fights. Tries to flee. Nowhere to go. Loses the fight quickly. Gown a noose. Claws dig into her bare shoulder.

Another match flares. Black bugs dart back and forth across white eyeballs. A huge, hooded head looms over Benni Lucretzia. Heavy legs straddle her. Bed too small. Bed's caving in. Elbow digs into her breast. She squirms free enough to kick, to pedal her legs furiously. Going nowhere. Hard hand over her mouth muffles her scream. Takes her breath away. She can't shout her daughter's name. *Elena. Hide, run, Elena.*

She stops twisting and flopping. She's pinned to the bed. A great weight crushes down. Stone hand cuts off breath. Don't kill my baby. Please. Please. Baby inside me. I won't fight. Won't run. Tiny heels kick, kick inside her all day long. Don't scare the baby.

Mountain sits where it wants to sit. Speaks her language. *Bianchi. Tedeschi, Tedeschi.* Rides her. Yanks her nightdress up to her shoulders. Fistful of hair he pulls if she bucks and twists. *Fiky, fiky. Lavorare.*

Another flash freezes the shape above her. Black an instant before white light blinds her. Hands grip her legs, stretch her wide open. She's being torn to pieces. She bites down on her tongue. The big one on top grunts. He's inside her. She lets him. Lets him stay. *Run Elena. Run.* Too tired to fight. Lets him. No fight left. Is the baby asleep. Don't hurt my baby.

Where are you, Elena. Light bright as day an instant then black as storms on summer nights. Elena's legs a blur behind Frieda's pale blur. Elena hides under the bed. Black wolf after her. No. No. Please. Let it be Frieda. Frieda down there on the floor eaten by a wolf. *Lavorare. Lavorare.* Where is she, Frieda. Is my baby dead. Where is my daughter.

Fred McMurray, Louis Till's codefendant, hanged with Till on July 2, 1945, near Aversa, Italy, testified to CID agents on July 19, 1944: "After we were inside, Till and the English soldier both said, 'fiky-fiky' to the women who were inside. The two (2) who were in the front room said, 'sì.' One of them caught me by the hand and the other caught the English soldier by the hand and both said: 'Vieni Qua.' The old man was lying across the foot of the bed crying, so we all went into the back room where we found another woman in bed. Thomas asked this woman to 'fiky-fiky' and she said 'sì,' so she and Thomas went into the front room. The woman I had got in the bed and pulled up her dress. I got on the bed and was trying to get my rod out. Just as I got my rod out, Till came up to me with his cock in one hand and the .45 automatic in the other. He told me to get up and after a little argument I did as he said because I was afraid of him (Till is bigger than I am and he also had the gun on me). The Englishman was fucking his woman on the floor so I went back to the front room where the old man, Thomas and his woman were . . . Till, Thomas and the English soldier all got some tail, but I didn't. The English soldier stated that he was laid twice."

Drunk soldiers tripping over each other hurry through the door of a shack in Civitavecchia. The door's flung open from inside while they stagger slow motion, sneaking around outside, then suddenly they are inside, Alice through the looking glass.

For an hour they had sat on a stone wall. Vino. Talked, laughed. Vino. Planned. Vino. Talked. Vino. Crept through weeds to get closer to the shack, close to doing something they didn't know exactly what. Just talk. Just mouth. Just Vino. Creep and crawl so nobody sees them. Then the sky lit up like Fourth of July. They're inside now. It's pitch dark and now they know what they're going to do next. Everything they big and bad enough to do.

It's one of the women from inside who opens the door, sees them, scoots back into the dark shack. None of the men know the woman's name is Frieda Mari. They chase her. Push. Grab. She owns no name. Men don't know their own names. They know women stay here. In this barracks where guys buy vino. Where some niggers lying or maybe not lying claim they buy pussy. Two women and a skinny little girl almost a woman. Close enough to woman to fuck. As they go up and down the Waterpoint hill to the Italian soldiers' camp for vino when no vino to be copped down below, they often see women around the shack. Women washing clothes. Hanging up GI khakis to dry. Two short, thick heifers. Not pretty. Pussy. Pussy's pussy. A girl outside sometimes. Girl pussy.

The men are drunk enough to say, Why not. Cop some. Buy. Take. Whatever. We're soldiers, goddamnit. War, damnit. U.S. Army don't take no for no answer. Soldiers take. *Fiky. Fiky.*

An old man fights them. Beat him down in a second. An old, old woman too old to fuck screams, falls on top the old man who's knocked out cold on the bed.

Dark. Can't see a goddamn thing. Two women in here somewhere. Not old. Not young. There's one. A girl. She hollers. Runs. Get her. Light a match, man. Hurry up. Light this motherfucker up.

Buy. Take. Do what you said you were going to do. Or didn't say. After you finish the vino Till copped up the hill, you sit and talk on the stone wall alongside the road. Pussy. Houseful. Vino bout gone. Cop more. Buy. Take. Get me some. Young girl in there I wants. Fresh meat. Get me some that. Buy. Take. Drunk men sit and drink and scheme a plan to cop and the shack door pops open in their faces. Plan was hoods, masks, some go in the front door or through a hole in the roof. Some in back door, except no back door. Front door blows open. Blows plan. Dark inside. Now what you going to do. Do what. You can do whatever the fuck you want to do. Do it.

Woman in bed. Wake her up. Wake the fuck up. Work time. Time to go to work. Vino. *Fiky. Fiky.*

Work.

Nobody knows who. *We're white, not colored. We're Germans. Germans.* Drunk men doing their business. Hoods so nobody sees. Nobody knows. Do what they came for. What. Who said so. Who says no. Who got money. Who said stop. Who's chicken. Who ain't gon do what they said. What they supposed to do. Buy. Sell. Take. In the very dark hard to tell. Who. Black masks. Gun in your pocket shoot off your balls. Ha ha ha. In the dark. Who's who. Hee-hee. Ha-ha. You do what you came for. Nobody's business who. Boo-hoo. Shut the fuck up. Work. *Fiky-fiky.* You know who. We Germans. *White.* Tedeschi. Do it. Do it.

Then afterwards, they split up. Two of them, two drunk soldiers go shoot holes in somebody's door who won't give up no wine, no trim. Blam-blam-blam, you dead. Told you so. Shot that door good. Next time I tell them something they know I mean business. Blam-blam. Bet they some scared motherfuckers behind there.

Woman inside. Bullet in her belly. Crawls outside. Somebody drags her back inside. Dead.

I was not there. I am not Louis Till. Not Mamie Till. I'm guilty of imagining pictures, sounds, words. Mine. I make them up. They could or could not be the way. It happened. Truth.

Or you could say that it begins with sugar. Several colored soldiers had attempted to sell thirteen ten-pound bags of stolen sugar at La Cisterna, a.k.a. the Waterpoint, near Civitavecchia, on June 24, 1944. Investigation of the sugar theft eventually produced four suspects: Private William S. Hite 32113851, 176 Port Company; Private John (NMI) Kitchen 0877239, 175 Port Company; Private James Thomas, Jr. 16098325, 177 Port Company; and Private Louis (NMI) Till 3632273, 177 Port Company, all of 379th Port Battalion, APO 765. During interrogation Private Kitchen quickly turned, admitting his knowledge of the sugar theft scheme and implicating the other three suspects. Till, Thomas, and Hite chose to remain silent. They were released then reconfined in July to Military Police Headquarters while rapes and murder investigated.

* * *

In the course of investigating the theft of a .45 revolver from a U.S. Navy officer and the murder of an Italian woman, both occurring near La Cisterna aka Waterpoint on the same night of June 27–28, CID agents learned that two Italian women might have been raped that same night. CID prisoner William Hite, a suspect being held for the theft of thirteen bags of sugar, confessed his participation in the sugar deal but denied his involvement in the events of June 27–28. Agents indicated to Hite that reliable sources had informed them he was implicated in the crimes of June 27 and 28, and reminded him that death is the penalty for assaulting and robbing a naval officer, rape and murder of Italian citizens. Hite changed his story. He related his conversation with Private Thomas that occurred on the morning of June 28 in which Thomas bragged of stealing a .45 pistol from a "smart-guy-sailor" and "fucking" two Italian women the previous night. Hite said Thomas placed himself, Private Louis Till, Fred McMurray, and an unidentified British soldier in the vicinity of La Cisterna on the night of June 27. Finally, Hite reported that the day following his conversation with Thomas, Thomas pointed out to him a woman washing clothes outside one of the shacks clustered around the waterpoint. Thomas claimed he'd "fucked" her, Hite said. The house Thomas indicated to Hite and Hite indicated to investigating officers is the Mari residence, scene of the beatings and rapes. It sits a short walk from the dwelling where Anna Zanchi, an Italian civilian, was shot and killed.

Greetings:

Just to be sure it receives your attention, I'm forwarding directly to you a copy of the second statement from Private James Thomas, Jr., dated and sworn 18th July 1944, and attached as enclosure #1. Please include this statement with the first Thomas statement (5 July) sent to you in the packet of materials (CID report #41) from Lieutenants Rousseau and Herlihy, CID/RAAC, who took over the investigation of the crimes of 27/8 June near Civitavecchia. This statement corroborates circumstantial evidence gathered thus far by Rousseau and Herlihy.

The second Thomas statement is exactly what's needed to hang Till and McMurray. We all know Till and McMurray guilty as hell. Vicious animals who deserve hanging. No doubt Thomas just as bad, a liar who would offer a third statement contradicting the first two if he believed it could save his black ass. However, if Thomas is charged as a codefendant, the value of his testimony at trial would be diminished. I suggest we remove Thomas from the indictment. Offer him clemency if he cooperates. No way we can totally clean up Thomas for the court, but if we don't indict him, it will work better for our side.

I suggest also that neither Thomas statement be included in the materials you forward to defense attorneys. I haven't heard yet who will be assigned the scummy job of defending Till and McMurray. Whoever it is doesn't need a preview of the Thomas statements. This case is cut and dry. No reason to complicate matters by offering grist to the mill of some showboater or hotshot or bleeding heart who will use any excuse to prolong court-martial. A review board will be happy to confirm a guilty verdict even slightly in conformity with the law. Everybody's aware we have a war to finish up. You read Ike's memo, didn't you? Why waste a minute on these animals.

If we drop Thomas, I'm sure I can convince Till and McMurray to be tried jointly—saving the government and us lots of headaches. So let's drop Thomas. His testimony will convict McMurray and Till, sure thing. Without a murder weapon and no positive ID from any of the victims, I'd say hanging two out of three guilty monkeys not a bad score. I'm still sweating McMurray. I'll tell him Till is ratting on him. After I read McMurray the second Thomas statement, my guess is McMurray will blame everything on Till. Being scared will make McMurray more stupid than he already is, and McMurray's story will cook his own goose, along with Till's.

(P.S. Let's have a drink when you're in town.)

The letter quoted above is not in the Till file. Why would it be. It's not the sort of letter that would be included in the official record of a court-martial, especially one whose result is a double hanging. Or perhaps the letter does exist, inscribed with invisible ink between the lines of letters the Till file treats as appropriately impartial, routine, fair. Letters forwarding the usual business of a court-martial. I include an agent's fictional letter to animate a meaningful silence, fill in a significant space the file leaves blank. Army officers in charge of Louis Till's case in 1944–45 wouldn't need to write down what they thought of Till nor what they intended to do with him. Without putting a word on paper, each officer could communicate his sentiments quite accurately to his colleagues. A quick phone call, lunch in the officers' club, a wink, a nod, a handshake would suffice. Till's case was decided just as surely by what transpires off the record as by what's on the record. What's the difference. Written in stone. Written in the wind.

* * *

Louis Till understood officers and gentlemen. He understood the code whose uniforms and insignia they wore. Till's silence in their presence is not ignorance or fear, but proof of his unspeakable clarity. He sees the DTC's circle of stout poles bristling with coils of barbed wire, sees gun towers rimming the stockade. Beyond his cell he hears voices, barks, grunts, drums, whistles, bugles, whinnying horses, *thwat*s of an officer's big stick across some fool's back. He hears the prophecy of his guilt drawing closer each day, as he never doubted it would.

Till knows that the language of officers and gentlemen asks for no response. Should I argue Till's silence was a mistake. What can someone like me, a fence straddler, fence climber, scrambler-up of unsurmountable stone walls, teach Louis Till. So I forge a letter. As if I've made it over the top, as if I'm ensconced inside the circle of officers and gentlemen. Fair. Fair enough. Fair because sooner or later I will lose my grip, slide back down where I'm supposed to be. Next to Till. Me and Louis. Louis and me. Till death do us part.

Fair. When are facts fair. In a not fair world where facts are fictions, how could facts be fair. Why would they want to be. Even if they tried to be. In spite of such questions, I begin at the beginning. Read the file one more time. To be fair. To seek facts. To mix facts and fiction into something fairly believable.

Till's crime is a *crime of being*, I decide after spending hours and hours one afternoon, poring through the file, an afternoon not unlike numerous others, asking myself how and why the law shifted gears in its treatment of colored soldiers during World War II. Asking why colored men continue to receive summary or no justice, a grossly disproportionate share of life sentences and death sentences today. Whether or not Till breaks the law, his existence is viewed by law as a problem. Louis Till is an evil seed that sooner or later will burst and scatter more evil seeds. Till requires a preemptive strike.

A fair person might interject that Louis Till's capital conviction was scrutinized by three separate boards of review, a process strictly adhering to army regulations. A vetting at least as thorough as most death penalty convictions receive today. Didn't colored Louis Till enjoy every legal benefit of the doubt to which any citizen is entitled. In response to this fair interjection, I offer a phrase from one of my favorite novels, *Sula*, describing how a guy in the Ohio town of Medallion copulates with a woman he intends to abandon first thing next morning: *with the steadiness and intensity of a man on his way to Akron.* A funny, disturbing line even though I never could exactly figure out if the fucking was good or bad, fake or authentic. Probably all of the above, Ms. Morrison winks. In Till's court-martial as in the case of that fuck in a bed in Ohio, all the details are managed scrupulously—every *t* crossed, every *i* dotted. But seamless, careful, by the book performance provides no evidence of what the spider's thinking about the fly enmeshed in its web.

Justice defeated and denied each time it goes through the motions and mistreats Louis Till. *Equal Justice* for *all* a coin, and I flip it. For an instant, airborne and spinning, the coin indeterminately heads and tails, simultaneously both and neither. A shining emblem of fairness. Then the coin lands, one face displayed. Unimpeachable, impartial. You win or lose. Sunny-side up. Or down. Justice may be cruel, but *amen*—same Justice for all. Then I turn the coin over, see its hidden face is the twin of the face that came up on top, the face that buries Till's face beneath its serene smile.

I continue to experience a kind of vertigo as I read and reread the trial record sent by the Virginia archive. Its contents shift, deny mastery of even simple matters—who said what, when, where. Each reading slightly twists the kaleidoscope, tumbles colors and shapes into new configurations, scrambling, erasing patterns, I've observed. Paginating my copy of the file—a penciled number at the bottom center of each white-bordered, yellowish gray sheet had not helped. Meaning expressed by the sequence of pages is as elusive as the page's color. The color I'd call *gray* if I had to choose a name for it today. The color I'd once imagined as parchment, then mummy-wrap in my flights of fancy. The original pages had simply grayed as they aged in the archive—grayed like me—like gray fuzzing my noggin before the barber crops it, like my gray, stubbled cheeks in the morning, gray like the wrinkled scrotal sac I lift to examine a suspicious, itchy pimple while I sit on the toilet, bathed in the merciless glare of fluorescent tubes above a mirror above the sink.

Because I'm hopelessly superstitious, afflicted by a kind of old school supernatural respect and yearning for authenticity, for purity, I don't try to resolve my quarrel with the sequence of pages by the obvious expedient of removing the supersize flat staple which binds the file, freeing the pages, reordering them however I see fit. I wouldn't attempt to explain to any rational human being just exactly what it is about the present state of my copy of the file that makes it special. Nor why tampering with the copy I received would be evil.

Yes. I could duplicate my copy and store the original somewhere safe to preserve whatever precious qualities I believe it possesses. But duplication would require dismantling the original and a careless clerk or my clumsy hands or a berserk machine might alter the sequence of pages or eat one or double one or forget one. Once disturbed, the authentic copy would cease to exist, and all the king's horses, all the king's men couldn't put it back together again.

Frustration of a different sort dogs my efforts. No matter how efficiently I maneuver through the file, I won't find Louis Till. Till is not asleep in there, waiting for my magic wand. Why would he break his silence, even if I discover his hiding place in the document's layers and layers of words. He's lost like his son Emmett returning to Chicago inside boxes of metal and wood. Like remains of colored American soldiers boxed, transported to dishonorable holes in France. Father like son like father. Till ghosts coming and going, and I'm helpless as Mrs. Till who stands in the Twelfth Street Station. Mamie Till deep within the profound quiet inside herself, listens, waits, hopes to pick out from the muted roar of trains arriving, trains departing, the whistle of the engine that brings her murdered boy back to life.

* * *

On the file's last page, in a clean space below typed words and above the canceled *confidential* stamp, I tag the file with fragments from the locked-up poet's cantos.

and Till was hung yesterday
for murder and rape with trimmings
. . . thought he was Zeus ram or another one

"St. Louis Till" as Green called him. Latin!

and those negroes by the clothes-line are extraordinarily like
the figures del Cossa

III

GRAVES

Even in death, no rest for Emmett Till, the Associated Press headline announces. As part of yet another investigation of his murder, Emmett Till's body had been exhumed four years previously to verify through DNA testing that the corpse returned from Mississippi to Chicago in 1955 was indeed Till's. Turns out Till's body (now scientifically certified as his) may not have been properly reinterred. The glass-topped casket ordered by Mamie Till—*so the world can see what they did to my baby*—was discovered "in a rusty shed at a suburban cemetery where workers are accused of digging up and dumping hundreds of bodies in a scheme to resell burial plots. The casket, which was seen by mourners around the world in 1955, was surrounded by garbage and old headstones. When authorities opened it, a family of possums scampered out . . ."

The article reports that according to cemetery officials, Emmett Till's original, glass-lidded casket had been stored in a shed because it was being saved to become part of a national civil rights memorial. Officials also claim that Till's body was placed in a new casket that lies buried in a section of the cemetery undisturbed by the perpetrators of the grave-robbing, grave-selling scam. Till family members are said to be considering another exhumation in order to be sure the body in the new casket is Till's.

* * *

In 1941 when I was inside her belly, my mother, because her skin was very light in color, could sneak me into the more comfortable, cleaner, *whites only* section of Washington, D.C., movie theaters. She said she was scared each time she smuggled us in but tied a scarf around her nappy hair and risked it, she said, on those infrequent occasions a spare dime was available to take in a matinee. She believes my father on one of his rare afternoons off from his government job, could have performed the same trick by walking up boldly, confidently, dressed in an African-looking robe and turban to a movie house ticket window and requesting a reserved seat. A colored D.C. man she'd read about in *Jet* had gotten away with it, so why not my father, she insisted, even with his brown skin and mine colored like his if it happened to show through whatever my father wrapped me in to carry me in his arms. Years later, after our family had migrated north from D.C., my mother recounted the sneaking into a movie scenario and I offered no comment, though I was dead certain the masquerade she had proposed, successful or not, would have given no satisfaction to the man I knew my father was.

I put Louis Till in my father's place in my mother's story. Louis Till carrying Emmett, father and son both African regal in bright swirls of colorful cloth. Stealing my father's very polite waiter's voice a minute, Louis Till requests a seat on the reserved ground floor, please. Flashes a smile at the young white woman in the ticket booth. She doesn't meet the gaze of the turbaned, robed man. Instead, her eyes drop to supervise fingers invisible to Louis Till, below the barred oval of window in the yellowish lit booth, fingers that should be punching an order into the ticket machine but don't. While she hesitates, the attendant raises her eyes to peek at the face, dark as my father's or mine, a face she's certain does not belong in the section where whites only are supposed to sit and view the screen. Hesitation lasts long enough for her to recall *yes,* she did get a good look at the face before she averted her eyes, and *yes* she had seen a color that warned her fingers *hold it, not so fast, look again,* and *yes* she did pause, look again and see dark color again. Now the white smile splitting very brown skin has vanished, replaced by something not quite a snarl, more like a warning low in an animal's throat, less an audible noise than a silence vibrating in her guts as the creature's eyes regard her across a chilling distance that's also chilling proximity. How does he stay a step ahead of her. How does she sense in advance what he will do. Her eyes fall quickly to the level of her hands once more. Watch the machine dispense the reserved ticket the man has demanded. She anticipates a smile, though a different kind this time, will reappear when she lifts her eyes and she will ignore it. Just push the ticket through the slot into which his dark hand pushes money, and then it will be all over. She will have kept her eyes to herself, not on the stolen ticket, not on brown fingers raking in change the machine owes. Coins clink down the chute, *clink, clink, clink,* landing in a metal dish half outside the booth. Half safe inside.

I flew to France to find Louis Till's grave. My French wife was jealous but it was impossible just then on short notice for her to accompany me. Bought my ticket the last day before a special round-trip offer expired. I'd noticed the cheap fare in a newspaper, cut out the ad and taped it conspicuously on the fridge, tempting myself for weeks, right up to the day before the offer's deadline. A last-minute decision to go left almost no time to warn old friends I needed a place to stay and hoped they could put me up a few days in their Paris apartment. Starting day after tomorrow, I apologized over the phone and Chantal laughed. Of course, no problem, always happy to see you, et cetera, saying in her impeccable English all the nice things good friends are supposed to say. She also informed me that Antoine was preparing for an important show and they both would travel soon to Nice for the opening. My second day in Paris, in spite of his hectic schedule, the tension of exhibiting new work, Antoine drove me one hundred–plus kilometers to Oise-Ainse and back for a quick visit to the American Cemetery and Memorial where I expected to find Louis Till's grave. We found it and returned to Paris in time for a late dinner in a restaurant with Chantal.

Louis Till's grave subdued me. During the car ride from Oise-Aisne to Paris, and later in the restaurant. I had no desire to speak about Till or anything else. Told only one Till tale that night, and not until a waiter had refilled our glasses from a second bottle of good Bordeaux and I noticed Chantal was not being her usual voluble, flirty self. I didn't want her to believe my silence about finding Louis Till's grave meant I was excluding her because she missed the trip or worse, believe I was treating the Till business as strictly man business I intended to discuss only with Antoine.

My abrupt arrival alone, suitcase in hand, into the midst of busy preparations for Nice, had allowed us very little time to catch up with much of anything personal. This was fortunate, in a way. I couldn't explain to myself why I felt compelled to rush across an ocean to visit a dead man, so how could I explain to my friends my sudden appearance at their door. A bit of background information about the Tills, father and son, was the best I could offer, plus an awkward admission I was following a plan whose shape and intent remained mysterious to me, a plan that evolved as it invented itself step by step, me in tow. The steps were clearly necessary, as I performed them, though I had not anticipated or consciously prepared for them nor could I guess what the next step might be or where it would lead. Fortunately, both my hosts had long been smitten by a very French love of blues, jazz, and gospel, and when I finally hit upon the word *improvisation* in my uneasy ramble, they both mercifully nodded and smiled.

In the restaurant, two of us fresh from the Oise-Aisne trip she'd been forced to miss, a trip she understood was urgent for me, Chantal's good sense and good manners prevented her from asking questions. I knew she had to be more than curious. I owed her and definitely didn't want her to feel left out, so I broke my silence about Louis Till's grave as best I could under the circumstances. Described a recent truth-stranger-than-fiction news item, replete with blackly humorous details about grave stealers and a family of possums residing in an abandoned, glass-topped coffin.

After I finished the anecdote gleaned from the Internet, Antoine volunteered to drive me to the cemetery again, first thing after they returned from Nice. I thanked him and hoped aloud Chantal would be free to make the trip. She smiled at me, and suggested that Antoine offer the keys to his family's holiday cottage in Brittany, just in case I might prefer a few days of rural peace and quiet to bumping around in hectic Paris while they were away in Nice. Yes of course, he said. I gratefully accepted both offers. I didn't tell them I welcomed the chance to hide away more than I relished the prospect of revisiting the cemetery. I needed downtime. I'd found Louis Till's grave. Stood next to it. Now what. I caught a train to Brittany the morning my friends drove south. We agreed to rendezvous in five days at the Paris apartment, and two days after that I would be on my way back to the States, my wife, all the time allotted by my special excursion fare exhausted.

Surrounded by fields and woods, the cottage near the Gulf of Morbihan sat private and isolated, a forty-five-minute walk from Arradon, the closest town. Arradon a town where years later my wife and I would buy a house. Train from Paris to Vannes, bus Vannes to Arradon, taxi from town to cottage, Antoine's family name as he'd promised, enough of an address for the taxi driver to deliver me.

I imagined the cottage must be centuries old. Huge chimney and a steeply sloped thatch roof like an oversize, beat-up straw hat pulled down snugly atop its stone walls. An outer wall of stone enclosed the cottage and its small garden. The sort of dwelling I remembered from pictures in fairy-tale books my mother read to me. Except there was no family of bears to greet me when I unlocked the front door, switched on the lights in rooms whose shuttered windows and doors sealed out the afternoon sun. The interior of the cottage was compact, efficient, tidy, with rooms all on one level except for a tiny loft in one corner, more bird nest than room. The ceilings high, beams exposed. Plank floors and wood-paneled walls gave it a warm feel. Casual, miscellaneous furniture, sturdy and indestructible. Bric-a-brac, knickknacks, prints, and paintings everywhere. The presence of previous visitors is so palpable I felt obliged to announce myself, new guest in residence, just passing through, folks. Anxious not to do anything that would spoil the next person's stay. I promise to dispose of garbage, leave floors broom clean, bathroom scrubbed, and when I depart, rest assured, everybody, all my stuff will leave with me.

About forty-eight hours before I introduced myself to an empty house, I had been standing alongside Louis Till's grave, a stay in a picturesque cottage unanticipated. No future is conceivable in Plot E. Only endless, gray repetition, unhappy flashbacks collapsing into more unhappy flashbacks. No excitement. Not a glimmer of satisfaction when I'd reached Till's grave. Nothing to cushion the fall. *What did you expect, turkey.* I'd been in Plot E before, in a book, and that visit had prepared me for Till's absence, for Plot E's smothering quiet, the neatly trimmed grass, numbered stones. But I had not foreseen the palpable presence of Till's enemies. Their thoroughness, implacability. Louis Till unable to shed them even after death.

In Brittany as I decided, among other things, whether or not to return to Louis Till's grave, I spent lots of time with my mother. She walked beside me. I heard her voice. Remembered how much I missed her, and that loss made me remember missing other family members. My uncle Eugene for instance, my father's younger brother killed by a sniper's bullet as he and his buddies beachcombed for souvenirs on the island of Guam in September 1945, a few weeks after Japan had surrendered and victory declared in the Pacific. Though his body, like the body of Louis Till, never made it home after the war, my uncle had not surfaced in my Till file ruminations until my mother talked about Eugene in Brittany.

My mother had never accepted my claim I possessed recollections of my uncle apart from stories I'd heard about him. I remain positive that I saw him live once, balancing himself on one long leg then the other, as he tugs off giant sneakers and tosses them into the closet just inside the front door of my grandmother's house. *Boy, you know you better not come in my clean house with those stinky dogs on your feet.* I believed I had heard those words. Saw shoes on my uncle Eugene's feet. Saw him loosen the laces and kick his sneakers off. Eugene grinning down at me as each one landed *clunk* in the closet.

My mother conceded I might recall seeing Eugene's shoes, but empty shoes she's sure. Eugene's sneakers sat in the back of the hall closet gathering dust because my grandmother refused to accept the fact her son Eugene, alive—*Hallelujah*—in his letter celebrating the war's end, wasn't coming home. The yellow telegram from the government had to be a mistake. Grandma forbid everybody, on pain of death, to touch Eugene's shoes, so I may have seen his shoes and heard stories about his big, funky feet, but not until after the war, when we moved north from D.C. and I was grown enough to begin remembering things. Afterwards she said, that's what I was remembering. Too young to recall Eugene before he left, underage himself, in a big hurry in 1943 to go fight the war.

My mother had plenty of stories about the years my father was away in the war and we lived with my mother's parents, John and Freeda French, my light-skinned grandparents. In Brittany I recalled my mother's memories of my brown-skinned grandmother's inconsolable grief. Grandma waiting, waiting for word of Eugene, her missing son, my father's brother. She said she was watching for the postman, but everybody knew it was Eugene she waited for at the gate of the knee-high, rusty iron fence in front of her row house's thumbnail of yard.

My father's mother grew enormous yellow roses, and shared cuttings from them with neighbors. On my trips home from college, years later after she died, I'd see her when I passed big bunches of yellow roses in other people's yards. My grandmother at the mailbox beside the gate every morning for ten years till she was too crippled up by a stroke to make it on her own down the short, brick path. Too proud and bitter to ask for help. Year after year, every single day for ten years, my mother said. Not one day missed, rain or shine, sickness or health. But my mother may have been exaggerating. My mom not always totally accurate. Not always right. About me and Uncle Eugene, that's one good example, probably. But, anyway, it was mostly my mother's stories, her voice, keeping me company in Brittany's quiet.

Brittany's quiet seldom silent. Seldom empty. From high overhead on wires that delivered power to the cottage, touterelles coo-cooed from dawn to dusk. Each searching, solitary cry perfectly echoed all the others. Cries that did not break stillness but enlarged it. Cries endlessly announcing and lamenting loneliness, whether or not coo-cooing aroused another touterelle's response. The large, pigeon-like birds also played hide-and-seek inside thick foliage above the garden walls, rustling leaves with swift, busy bouts of lovemaking. Invisible sea and wind always present in the quiet. If I shut my eyes I would hear the faraway rumble of waves crashing, shrieks and caws of gulls.

At night the wooden walls, floors, and ceilings of the cottage expanded and contracted, perhaps to accommodate the weight of dreams passing back and forth, unfinished dreams left behind by previous visitors. Brittany's busy stillness night and day a relief of sorts, different from the silence of Louis Till's wordlessness. Then again not so different either. In eloquence. In effect. If I meet Louis Till eye to eye, and he chooses not to utter a single word, I would understand that I was being addressed by his silence. Understand that much more than words at stake.

In Gare Montparnasse on my way to Brittany, as I had waited for a train to Vannes, my eyes happened to settle on a stranger, a man with nothing special about him who passed by close enough to touch, a man going in the opposite direction through a crowded underground corridor. For an instant his gaze crossed mine. Caught looking, we both performed the urgent, slapstick, head-snapping look away, as if we were guilty of something, or suspect at least. Guilty of what. Looking or looking away. Guilty of curiosity. Fear. Secrets. Why so uneasy in the mirror of another's eyes. Even when another's gaze engages only an instant. Louis Till's gaze is not shy. He refuses to look away. Silence is Louis Till's briar patch. His ground zero. Till does not break the silence of exchanges with him. Scorns words. Till's naked self in my naked eyes, mine in his.

On the same day of the guilty encounter in Gare Montparnasse, I watched the French countryside unfurl between Paris and Vannes, a tapestry of orderly strips of green, brown, black outside the TGV window, and tried to imagine Louis Till's silence forming around things he observed. Till mapping an inner landscape he can move through efficiently, wordlessly. Guide others through it if he chooses. Or let others think whatever the fuck they want to think about what he's thinking. Till hears words spoken or unspoken by others, then decides whether the words belong in his world. He's probably correct that silence works better than speech to test whose world exists—Till's world out there huffing, puffing to bust down the door, barge in and eat him or eat the world another person's words invent. Silence is a game of chicken. Don't flinch. Winner takes all.

Mile after mile of rich land basking under bright sunlight rolls placidly by the train window. Operating-room-clean orchards drop no fruit to litter the grass. Perfect copies of perfect specimens of cows, goats, sheep, horses in place, copies that don't need to move or move their bowels or be fed. Why would anyone insist anything should change. What could be better than this, this way it seems the French countryside has always been, always is. Maybe I should leave Till's dry, old bones alone. No sign Louis Till was happy to see me when I showed up at his grave. No high five. No hug. No grin.

Before France, before I began to grasp how little or how much of Louis Till's story could be retrieved, before I understood I would need more than a lifetime to acquire the little or the lot, not to complete a Till project, just to tease it forward a useful inch or so, I rode a bus south to look for information about James Thomas, Junior. If any single voice guaranteed a noose would settle around Louis Till's neck, it could have been the voice of Junior Thomas, Till's buddy in Port Company 177, 379th Battalion, Transport Command. A voice rising from the welter of ghostly voices that had settled like dust on the Till file's yellow-gray pages I read again and again, dust on my fingers, in my eyes, nostrils as I sifted through the transcript asking dust to do what dust cannot do, assume shape, substance, breathe and speak again. On that trip south to research archives and public records, hoping I might discover something useful about Junior Thomas, about the south Louis Till's son Emmett had visited in 1955, I decided I would pay a quick visit to the graves of my father's side of the family in Promiseland, South Carolina, a pilgrimage, a duty I'd avoided far too long.

On the way south droning bus tires, drone of the interstate's interminable sameness, a peculiar combination of anticipation and dread kept me from dozing off, reminded me of my first return home from college. I'd worn a Senegalese boubou on a Trailways bus droning at night across the turnpike, Philly to Pittsburgh. My father had registered his disapproval of my tunic the instant I entered the front door of our Copeland Street house. Before I could cross the room to his chair, he made his opinion abundantly clear, dismissing my garment not with words, just a slow nod, eyebrows raised, lips pinched inside one corner of his mouth, head cocked to one side, cheek tensed, tilted the way he had held it up to shave difficult spots with his straight razor while I stood behind his back entranced, three or four foot tall, watching him through the open bathroom door gaze at himself in a mirror.

After my father's silent critique of my tunic, I made sure to don it each day of my stay. Then never wore it again in life. The boubou didn't return to school with me, discarded who knows where, though I thought about it, missed it on the three-hundred-mile ride back to my dorm room across Pennsylvania's empty mountains. Missed the coarse fabric, its ribs of raised stitching I liked to pick at, the faint, oddly sweetish funk inhabiting the tunic when I lifted it from a hanger in a West Philly shop. I often wondered if other people could smell it when they stood close to me. I missed its threads of many colors, colors to which I assigned the few African female names I'd heard, imagining hair, voices, eyes, lives for the women, for us, our bodies entwined, a dance of touches, scents, noises, warmth, weaving the boubou's bold, bright stripes.

My father's contempt is almost funny now, and I wish I could have smiled at him, let him see I understood he was not simply putting me down. Show him I was grown enough, smart enough to figure out some things on my own. Not always only about me, my tender ego, fragile vanity, my predatory youngblood self at the center of the universe. I wish I had possessed the courage to speak loud and clear to my father. No, Daddy. Yes, Dad. Say yes and no to my father and let him understand that I meant what I said. Why couldn't I say then what I would say now—You're always part of the picture, Dad. Picture is you, me, both of us and this whole precarious family in the shit together.

Whether I agreed with him or not about the appropriateness of draping myself with a particular piece of Senegalese cloth, my father had more than earned his right to pass a judgment. And why wouldn't he resent, disparage, even despise the sudden privilege I granted myself to distance myself from his world. Silent disapproval was not necessarily intended to chill me. Stop me in my tracks. Probably less a matter of trying to hurt my feelings than a reminder to respect his. His rights. His obligation to protect them. A son's obligation to honor a father's space. Both of us touched and hurt most by exactly what we could never talk about—things like why no silly tunics, no college for my father.

If I had responded differently to him both of us might have survived prickly exchanges with less regret, more grace, more peace. Laughing together later about moments which he himself, even back then, must have seen as at least partly humorous—his knucklehead son home from college wrapped up in some kind of Halloween costume bathrobe strutting around Pittsburgh's streets. Funny in a way, though also absolutely not amusing. Like fear of the south that sneaked back to tease me, haunt me on my journey below the Mason-Dixon Line to find facts about James Thomas, Junior.

For me, a colored kid growing up in the fifties in Pittsburgh, Pennsylvania, *South*, like Hollywood's Africa, was a distant, primitive region. Dark. Dangerous. Untouched by time. By history or progress. South was the home of savages not my color who would catch, cook and eat me, not welcome me back. I'd been cautioned never to trust those pale-faced southerners with their odd accents. Their ghost color. Ghost blue eyes. Beady black eyes with no pity. They mean you no good, the elders warned. Never have. Never will. And watch your step, boy. Plenty them up here in the North.

Boys who were teenagers, colored boys raised in northern cities like Emmett Till and me were only a generation or two removed from the old days, old ugly ways, old ugly country. We'd been taught in school and schooled daily by messages in the culture to believe we were not exactly Americans. More like orphans. Ancestors unknown. Except for cartoons of dumb, black slaves or Africans even blacker, dumber. And who wouldn't want to forget them.

Parents, grandparents, great-grandparents, old uncles and aunts remembered the south fondly in tales they recounted to each other and their progeny, down-home tales full of laughter, pats, hugs, dance steps, pantomimes, *mmmmm-mmmm* good food, clear air, clean water, black soil my Virginia grandfather, John French, said he believed sweet enough to eat when he was a boy staring at the Blue Ridge Mountains, daydreaming on the back porch of his father's house. Good hunting fishing funerals songs sermons weddings baptisms moonshine. Huh-uh. Forget about all that once-upon-a-time backwoods mess. Urban boys like me, like Emmett Till had heard other stories too.

I said, *No sir,* and *Thank you, Grandpa. Can't go this summer,* declining many summers my grandfather's invitation to accompany him south. Dodged a trip until Grandpa Harry, born in South Carolina and baptized Hannibal not long after slavery days, got too old to go and stopped asking. We missed the opportunity to travel together, hang out together in his briar patch, Promiseland. Grandpa was deprived of a chance to show off his grandson, first northern-born male child of the extended clan. Maybe Emmett Till took my place. Took my trip. Plunged into the jungle full of peckerwoods riding around in white sheets to hunt down black boys, cut off our balls, string us up. *Dixie, wish I was in Dixie.* No thanks, Grandpa. That Hannibal who after he settled up north, called himself Harry out of shyness or maybe shame because Hannibal sounded too much like Cannibal. I missed him on the droning bus south. Missed our golden summer together. Sorry, Grandpa. Wish you were here.

The U.S. Army's Disciplinary Training Center at Metato, near Pisa in Italy, where Louis Till was held prisoner, is a dark site like the south, like Africa, frozen outside of time. Another piece of alien territory where the Till project would land me. During World War II the DTC was a black hole. Colored soldiers made up twenty-five percent of the four thousand unlucky inmates at the mercy of white officers who ran the camp, by all reports, as if they were possessed by devils.

Uncountable miles away from the known, the everyday, the acceptable, the DTC an American prison on conquered Italian soil, a terrain ominous and unsafe for colored boys as any mythical Dark Continent, or the south. Colored inmates of the camp, exposed to bitter cold, withering heat, never-ending labor, humiliation, beatings, were born again slaves. White guards were vicious slave drivers in the DTC time warp. But if a famous American poet imprisoned with Louis Till was correct, a different Africa was also abounding in the Metato inferno. Luminous traces of dark speech, dark faces, dark music, the dark generosity of kind acts that dark hands dared to perform. Africa surviving but only if, like the poet, you paid attention, looked around yourself, inside yourself, and knew how to look. The poet's desk a gift from an African spirit disguised as a colored prisoner. A writing desk ingeniously fashioned from a packing crate just appeared one morning, no warning, in the poet's bare cell, compliments of quiet fellow prisoner Saunders, whose gleaming, bronze forehead, the poet wrote, belonged on a Benin mask.

Whereas the sight of a good nigger is cheering, wrote the captive poet, Pound, who plays Mistah Kurtz in my movie of the DTC camp, an endangered soul I must rescue, bring back alive as a witness for the defense to recite his *Pisan Cantos* at the court-martial of Privates Till and McMurray.

Ain' committed no federal crime,
jes a slaight misdemeanor

The DTC part of a story about James Thomas, Junior, began forming before I traveled south. It's likely that Private Thomas sees Private Louis (NMI) Till only once, if at all, after the court-martial in Leghorn, Italy. Sees him because a truck transporting Thomas and other recently released prisoners to rejoin their units probably routed through the MTOUSA (rhymes with Medusa) Disciplinary Training Center at Metato in order to pick up soldiers who had served out their terms there.

I peek through a hole where a loop of rope has come undone from one of the steel poles to which the truck's canvas sides and top are lashed, a missed stitch stretched wider for a merciful breath of air and probably also out of curiosity, too, since men sweating under the truck's canopy would want to check out the camp where they've halted, the granddaddy prison, largest and meanest of an archipelago of camps, a facility where some of them probably had been interned before. A place all of them certainly would have heard tales about. Hellish acres dusty and broiling in summer, bitter cold, wet and muddy in winter. DTC at Metato especially notorious because colored GIs attempting to escape had been machine-gunned by guards posted in one of the towers that jut up next to the gate and at each corner of the razor-wired perimeter fence.

Through the improvised peephole James Thomas sights a group of prisoners mustered at the far end of the DTC's football-field-long yard. This group gathered for a punishment not a work detail since the men's hands are empty and no tools are stacked nearby. To Thomas, who squints through the hole, the scene is a wobbly movie projected on a washboard. Men disintegrating in a buckling haze of heat, dust and glare, are colored men he guesses, like all the guys crammed in the truck, like the guys they wait for. He's certain it's a colored detail over there across the yard when a colored soldier double-times past to join the group. No mixed details in the DTC.

Thomas sucks air, drips sweat. Soldiers crowded beside him shove in slow motion, crabs in a barrel, silently, insistently squeezing closer to the privileged spot, the little riff of less stale air. For a minute his chance to look and breathe, breathe and look, but soon he'll have to shift, lose sight of men whose black silhouettes shiver and crack in the yard's heat.

Colored soldiers in rows over there face an officer who's white. Thomas knows he's white because all officers white. Baton in one hand, glint of silver whistle in the other. The whistle shrieks. Rows of men drop to the ground as if an invisible sickle slashed their ranks. All the prisoners, maybe twenty-five, thirty, freeze in the push-up position, a posture, a drill, a punishment way too familiar to Thomas. They are waiting for the whistle's next blast to commence the cadence count every man in the detail must shout at the top of his lungs. Loud enough to satisfy the officer or the whistle will throw a toot-toot shrieking fit, the count will go back to zero, the sentence of ten or thirty or fifty push-ups will start all over again. Hup-one-two-One-hup-one-two-Two-hup . . . All the troops mowed down except one. One sticks up like a hair the razor blade of whistle missed. For three or four counts two dark shapes stand face to face, white officer, colored soldier above rows of prone bodies that dip and rise in unison. Two silhouettes, too far away, too much hazy shimmer and glare to pick out features, but Thomas has no doubt one is Louis Till. Thick body, big head Till. Till ignores the count.

Till's upright like the officer. Meets the officer's stare. Matches hate for hate. Hate that would kill if it could. Thomas hears it hiss, catch fire. Like white heat from the blowtorches they used in the 379th.

Hate zaps back and forth three, maybe four beats while Till refuses to drop to the ground. Time enough for Thomas to think, *Gotta tell the fellas this shit. Till crazy, boy.* And Thomas wonders how many years he'll need to finish being a soldier, finish his life, finish with Louis Till.

Till, no doubt about it. Goddamn St. Louis Till on his feet after all the other men down. Till eye to eye with a peckerwood officer, hate traded for hate for an instant, an eternity before Till drops to his hands, arms extended under his chest, the push-up position held one beat, then two, his big head looking round side to side like what the fuck all this shit spozed to be, before he begins to pump up and down, up and fucking down. Hup-one-two-Six-Hup-one-two-Seven. Faster and faster, chasing shrieks of the officer's whistle chasing him.

Junior Thomas named names. Nods *Uh-huh. Louis Till.* Yes sir, he says again after the officer reads out Till's name and serial number. Yes, sir. Put on navy hoods and masks. Carried guns. Yes, sir. They busted in, fucked those Italian women at the Waterpoint. Yes sir. The Cisterna. Yes, sir, they did it. Till and them did just what you say they did and I didn't do nothing. No sir. Not me. Swear to God it was the others inside the shack done it and I didn't do nothing but watch. Just standing at the door but I could sorta see little corners of what's going down. Just like you say it happened. Yessir. Pulled the door shut behind me. Lit a match so I could kinda see. Dark in there. Had my back to the door where the four of us come in at. Yessir. Till, McMurray, the English guy go inside but I didn't go no further than the door. Four of us through the door, sir, not three like them Italian peoples say. They wrong, sir. Four not three. Them Italians inside the shack ain't seen me at the door, I guess. Cause I stopped. The others run in right away when the door opened. Went after the women in there, beat down the old man. But I stopped at the door.

First Till sent McMurray and the English guy, Chappie, we called him. No, sir. Never knew no other name. He call everybody *Chappie*, so we call him *Chappie*. Yes sir. Till said you two go round to the back and listen, check out who inside. McMurray come back said he heard what might be a man snoring and two, three women talking he said when him and the Englishman come back to where me and Till sat on the stone wall where we been sitting since dark, drinking vino. Four of us by the wall after McMurray come back with the English guy from sneaking up to the shack. McMurray said there's women in there, and Till said, C'mon then, said vino said pussy said raid. Louis Till don't talk much so when he says something you best listen. And do what he say do. Till's wild crazy. Got a .45 automatic in his pocket. Took it from a whiteboy sailor he punched out that night. Till snatched the .45 out the sailor's belt when the sailor reached for it. Knocked him down, stomped him, dared him to get up. Till just might have killed him if I didn't pull Till off. I saved that sailor boy's life. Let him be, man, I said. Nothing but trouble, I said to Till. Said, C'mon, man, let's go on up the hill to the Italian camp and cop some vino.

Till said raid and it's four us, not three, creep up on the shack. Then Pow. Boom. Boom. Guns, sirens, searchlights bright as day. Forty millimeters, nineties. Boom. Pow-pow-pow-pow. Shack door pops open.

* * *

Hey, Till. Don't roll your evil eyes at me, man. Bet you singing away, man. Fuck you, man. All you niggers singing. So fuck it. Fuck your evil eyes. I ain't the one started it. Hite started it. Hite tell the whole motherfucking world everything in his dumb, nappy head.

Don't roll those cold eyes at me. Leave me be, Till. Paper I signed ain't shit, man, just a couple, three words. Why you up in my face. G'wan away, Till. Somebody got to look out for James Thomas, Junior. Yessir. Zackly, sir. You got it, right, sir. What you say is surely what happened. I don't want to hang by the neck until I'm dead. Who do. Do you, Till. Goddamn that Hite.

Must be near morning before they bring the statement to sign. CIDs took a long break for dinner around five, six. Never mind he's hungry, too. Gone a good, long while then more questions soon's they come back. No lunch, no dinner, not a fucking Coke for him, just questions all night. Yessir, nosir, same shit over and over or different shit, no sir, yes sir, none of it making no damn sense no more. The more he says, the more he can't remember from one story to the next and the white boys pick, pick, picking at each story as if he knew, as if he cared. Like any bit of truth anywhere in any of it. Don't matter what the fuck he say or don't say. One story same as another. Like Till always said it don't mean shit no way. Tell the same lie or a different lie. Fuck it.

When they bring a paper to sign he play reads the words because they say read. Signs because that's what CIDs order Private Thomas to do. Second statement no hassle. Three weeks or so after the first statement another CID in charge and then another one who bops in a second at the end to sign on the line below the line Junior Thomas signs. Thomas in and out quick, too. At attention in front of the CID behind the desk. A fan moves the air, moves officer stink. No talk, talk, talky, talking. Minute all it takes the CID to say, We cleaned up your first statement, Private. You forgot a few things we put in. We took out a few things we know you don't want to say. Read it if you want to read it, but I've just told you everything you need to know.

Yessir. Thank you, sir.

Good. You're doing yourself a favor, Private. Sooner we finish this business, better it will be for everybody concerned. Herlihy, c'mon. Need your John Hancock. Right. Good. Dismissed.

I was not in the CID lieutenant's office. Nor anywhere else in the DTC. I'm reporting imagination as fact. Unscrupulous as any army investigator. Worse because I claim to know better. Want my fictions to be fair and honest. As if that desire exempts me from telling truth and only truth. The United States Army's not exempt either, even if the army's duty to win a war and keep peace after war a more admirable excuse than mine for bending facts, inventing truth.

What would have happened if Louis Till had spoken, denied James Thomas's story, challenged it when interviewed by CID agents. What if Till had accused his accuser, Thomas, in a sworn statement of his own. What if, during investigation of the sugar theft that became an investigation of rape, color, and murder, Till had scared Junior Thomas, shut him up with an evil stare or wasted him in a dark alley in Naples the moment Till caught the glint, the hangdog Iago smirk of complicity and betrayal in the eyes of Junior Thomas. The innocent, imploring look of determination and helplessness in the eyes of a man who's fallen hopelessly in love and understands he is not loved in return and that nothing the loved or unloved can do, good or evil to the other, will ever unknot unrequited love.

Let it go. Resist temptation. Don't announce the unhappiness of Junior Thomas like it's good news. No. Let poor James Thomas, Junior, dead or not, rest in peace. He's a man, not a lesson. Lessons aplenty every minute of every day of each person's life. Let each of us teach ourselves, speak for ourselves, fabricate our file of lies. No fiction of evil James Thomas on the gallows or Saint Louis Till on the cross can spare us.

Anyway, truth is that on my journey south to gather facts, the closest I got to Junior Thomas was the coincidence of a last name he shared with Money Thomas, a jitney driver I hired to show me around Promiseland, South Carolina.

When I asked a young woman behind the reception desk of Greenwood's Marriott Inn how to get to Promiseland, she told me she didn't know, almost as if she was not aware a place called Promiseland existed. While I stood staring out the motel's glass entrance at a parking lot and driveway, a porter in a Marriott vest came up behind me and whispered in my ear. *She know, mister.* I followed him outside and he repeats, louder this time:

She know. A local and she know how to get to Promiseland. They all know. Black gals. White gals like her, too. They all know.

Still got they white joints and black joints but nowadays they all got Shuggs, too. She know how to get to Sugars.

Is Sugars . . . Shuggs . . . in Promiseland.

Yes and no. No Promiseland no more. Not the way it once was. You got a row of raggedy shacks nobody lives in. Shuggs after-hours club out behind them. Old schoolhouse sits a little ways off and that's it, all that's left of Promiseland. Empty shacks, rusty railroad tracks, school, and some little bitty farms nobody works no more. So if you ask the whereabouts of Promiseland, some folks say Promiseland gone. Not on the state highway map what they mean. But everybody local knows about Promiseland, remembers Promiseland and could take you right to it. Some might wish Promiseland long gone and good riddance but it ain't. Little sign just up the road a piece from where we stand says Route 10. Take 10 to the right and before you know it you there, Promiseland. No sign telling you you there. You might easy could miss it. Not much to see. Ain't no mystery neither if you know how to look. Promiseland sit where it always sat. Don't matter they mark it on the state map or not.

See that red Dodge van. Fella in it my friend, Money Thomas. Know his way everywhere around here. Give old Money a couple dollars the man show you anything you want to see.

The day I checked out of Greenwood's Marriott and on a bus back north I realized I hadn't told anyone—including Money Thomas, who drove me to old Mount Zion and waited while I bumbled around in tall weeds and high grass behind the abandoned church—about my family roots in Promiseland. Why I didn't, I still haven't figured out. Still scared of the south. Cat got my tongue. Who knows. The point is I did not claim the family name that appears in the community's earliest records, years before Promiseland became a community with a name and a school, years before someone had the idea of breaking up the old Willis plantation into small parcels and giving away or selling the land cheap to newly freed slaves to farm, years before a rumored promise of forty acres and a mule for every ex-slave family got sidetracked by the state of South Carolina into a moneymaking scam to benefit local whites who had previously owned both land and human beings who worked it.

As far back as 1867, documents attest, a Robert bearing my family name had presented himself and registered his X at the polling place. This despite the fact that roads and voting sites were patrolled by vigilantes. Armed, hooded white men on horseback who vowed, *Never. Not here, nigger.*

My people were among the first in line during Reconstruction when a few scanty plots of the Willis plantation's worst land were doled out to former slaves, and some of my ancestors were among the very few who managed to hold on to their farms in spite of decades of punishing taxation, debt, intimidation and swindles organized to systematically restore the land and colored people who worked it to their former lords and masters. So why didn't I introduce myself as a homeboy. Say my family from down here. Say my grandfather Hannibal left Promiseland in 1898 and went north. Say I'm the prodigal son come back to hear your stories and tell you mine. Hey, cuz. Hi auntie and uncle and great-grandma and great-great-granddaddy. We's all kin folks. Who knows what went down here. After dark in these woods. Mama's baby, Daddy's maybe, names and blood ringing the changes generation after generation of marriages and coupling and whatnot. Some folks gone for good, some never left home, some mixed half-white, some mixed half-black, some return from faraway places to die, some die in faraway places. Nobody knows and who cares, so here I am, and youall my people.

But during the side trip to South Carolina, I didn't, couldn't say, I'm Promiseland people. Too late. My people gone. Drastically severed from me and me from them by time and circumstance. I could not speak to the living about my ties to Promiseland. I confessed only in the burial ground of old Mount Zion, the church my great-grandfather had pastored, his name on a plaque on new Mount Zion's door. Reverend Tatum drove a horse-drawn buggy to take the pulpit each Sunday, his impeccably dressed wife next to him on the buggy's wooden seat. Her Sunday bonnet famous because one time they hit a bump and the hat landed in a juniper bush, according to one of my grandfather Harry's stories.

At the edge of the woods behind old Mount Zion AME I found several gravestones that bore the family name. Three in particular. Sturdy, rough-hewn, broad-shouldered stones belonging to *Jordan, Baker, Foster,* my great-grandfather Tatum's brothers, my grandfather's uncles side by side among scattered graves of parents, wives, uncles, aunts, sisters, in-laws, cousins, neighbors. My people I had never met and never would because once upon a time I was too ashamed or too scared to come south with my grandpa and it's too late now. Harry's youngest sister's son, Littleman, was the last known survivor of the clan my grandfather had left behind in 1898, and Littleman (a.k.a. James), whom I'd met when he visited my grandfather up north, must be buried by now behind one little country church or another. My people in the ground behind Mount Zion only ones heard me say, *I'm back.*

I'm here. Overwhelmed by their silence greeting me, that's about everything my heart, my head let me confess.

In Brittany I converse with stones. Small stones, scarcely larger than gravel on the Gulf of Morbihan's beaches, prattle under my sneakers. Stones hundreds of times my weight, darkly furred by algae, stand offshore. A herd of massive animals black against the horizon's shimmer, their bellowing and moaning blended into the sea's dull roar.

Stonescapes are various as seascapes. So many stones and every one is different each time I pass. Never the same stone twice. An unending flow of information and my eyes, ears can't keep up.

I try to convince myself to be satisfied with my limited point of view, my small grip. My irrelevancy a mercy finally that allows me to slip in and out of stony exchanges and silences, languages of no words I know, streaming like half-remembered incidents stream inside my head. I pass by transparent, weightless through a particular stones's glance and never have before, never will again.

When my mother accompanies me, I tease her. Ask if her mother's mother mothered by a stone. Does her secret ancestry account for my grim, stony expression people often complain about. The slow hardening of my flesh inside and out, my impenetrability, stubbornness, stiff joints. Is it why a state of rest with no desire to move has become my body's deepest, purest pleasure. I walk my older man's walk beside the sea, fascinated as a kid, or to put it more accurately, fascinated as an old man who samples a boy's ancient astonishment, a boy stymied, intimidated by every form's restless hunger for change. Each form's failure to be what it's not. A boy observing a world more fragile and ephemeral than he is. But it's also a world hard as stone. Shy as a stone. Stones are shy. Remove a wet stone from its setting and it loses color as it dries. A reverse blush. Stones grow pale like my mother, like Helen of Troy after she's kidnapped and carried far from home.

Competing with stones for my attention, corpses of jellyfish wash up in great numbers on the gulf's rocky beaches. Jellyfish in many ways are the exact opposite of stones, until I recall the French word *méduse* for jellyfish and Medusa's glare that turned humans to stone. Then I smile. We're all family here. All orphans. Stones. Me. You. All of us, I tell jellyfish rotting where the tide strands them.

A plague of dead jellyfish. The large ones are called *lion's mane* by the British to honor a cluster of eight long tentacles trailing the fish like dreadlocks as they swim through the sea. The jelly-fish look like humongous puddles of spit or mucus coughed up onshore. If the sun's bright, you can peer through their skin at an odd conglomeration of pastel-hued pipes, valves, pumps, viscera, organized for locomotion, reproduction, breathing, feeding, stinging, digestion, roaming the oceans' depths. An ocean that for reasons unknown—Chantal would blame unseasonably warm water temperatures, Antoine argued unseasonable cold when I related what I'd observed—was vomiting jellyfish in great numbers, stranding them dying and dead, draped over stones, wedged between stones, mired in dark clumps of algae.

I measure one dead méduse with my just slightly longer than

twelve inch sneaker. A yard and a half circumference I calculated, then said hello and goodbye to the swelling carcass of a creature whose anatomy, like a giraffe's, seems strayed from another dimension. A bowl of jelly that looks as if it should quiver when I nudge it with my toe, but it's surprisingly dense, firm.

One morning I witnessed very young children in school uniforms attack an immense dead or near dead jellyfish. Visible fear and loathing were expressed in the face of a boy who first notices the body. His classmates gather around him and as soon as it becomes clear the ugly thing can't defend itself, a predictable escalation of bravery, excitement that rises to a frenzy of singsong chanting, hip-hopping dance steps. They prod with shoes, poke with sticks, pelt with stones, smash with rocks as large as they're able to lift. Why didn't I shout, *Hey, kids. Stoppit. Jellyfish relatives. Yours. Mine. Ours.*

Another day, close to sunset, an hour's steady hump still to go before I reach the cottage, sea a quicksilver radiance over my left shoulder, and in front of me the sky climbs and climbs. I lower my eyes and they are attracted by a something that turns out not to be a bright stone nor jellyfish gleam, but an orange rubber glove washed up by the tide. A single glove lying on the sand, palm up, rubbery fingers curled as if they held something invisible or had let go of something and retained its shape. I found myself daydreaming a hand inside the glove. Not a gory, severed hand like in horror movies at the Belmar show, a live hand like mine, a hand my color, not the glove's orange of an orange. Perhaps a hand with fingers wrapped around something it had never held but wishes for or something precious it held once and yearns to have within its grasp again. But this glove washed up on the beach can't hold or let go of anything except sand and grit that collects inside it. No soap opera, just a glove, an orange rubber or latex glove with no flesh and bone fingers inside, no wishes, no memories of being alive once or alive now, just a thing, an orange-colored thing the tide delivered and soon enough will take back.

In Brittany, I chop up the Till file like William Burroughs chopped up his fiction to make new stories, a method not unlike my mother's way of composing stories. I place fragments of Benni Lucretzia's testimony at the Till, McMurray court-martial into a box, shake them up, shake them out . . .

—these colored soldiers came in, all three of them were masked. One tall one and two small ones . . . Three niggers entered my house during the raid . . . One of them grabbed me by the mouth. Another grabbed my daughter by the head, they did not find my daughter . . .

They came to me and started to hit me. I was asking for my daughter. One had a pistol in his pocket while he was raping me. One of them lighted a match and my daughter got under the bed. They did not find my daughter so she was untouched . . . I did not know she was under the bed and was looking for my daughter . . .

<u>How many matches did they light.</u> *When they were on top of me, two. I don't know. I was crying. I was looking for my daughter.*

You were watching what was going on beside you. Yes, because I thought it was my daughter, and I was yelling, "Frieda, do you know where my daughter is" . . . While one was on top of me, he lit a match and I lifted up the mask and he hit me . . . Did the mask cover their eyes? I didn't take note of it because as soon as they entered I started looking for my daughter . . .

Were you watching those two people? I was watching there . . . and I was asking, "Have you seen my daughter?" I thought my daughter was in the same . . . Now how could you tell that these were colored people. They lit a match. From the face and from the hands. When they were lighting the matches I could tell and when they had their hand across my mouth . . . And you weren't much interested in what was going on around you. No, because I was struggling myself, and I was thinking about my daughter.

Were they all colored people. Two of them were dark and one seemed to be a little lighter-sort-of-a-mulatto, but it was dark. Do you know what color clothing he had on. No, because I was searching for my daughter and couldn't see . . .

They hit me in the forehead and on the mouth and on the shoulder, and I was black and blue, they tore off all my clothing, I was all undressed, and one was on top of me and striking me because I wouldn't open my legs. I was forced. I had to. I was weak. I couldn't do anymore the big one was on top of me and the other held my legs . . . Did you see his penis. Yes, I saw it. They put that thing in.

How far. All of it. All the way because the other was holding my legs. How long. In Italian it spurted . . . All of it in. They had their way. I had a miscarriage, the same morning . . . I had a miscarriage.

Hunches are another way of cutting up and splicing the Till file. For instance my hunch is that Benni Lucretzia's young daughter Elena was raped or sold the night of June 27. If this fact was discovered by CID investigators, they didn't report it. Why not. Maybe because it's not fact. It's my hunch. A hunch the file doesn't confirm. Or negate. If Elena Lucretzia, a juvenile, had been raped or bought or both wouldn't army agents welcome that information as one more evil deed to pin on Till and McMurray. Yes and no. More is not always better. More mess is not a better mess and the army's case is messy, all soft, gooey circumstantial evidence. Problematic at best. A case difficult to make without witnesses willing to nail down neatly, precisely specific facts the judges require for a death conviction.

Benni Lucretzia and Frieda Mari, according to CID agents, did not report immediately that they had been raped because they were frightened American soldiers might retaliate. The women also said they wished to avoid the public shame and humiliation of being rape victims. Similar fears of disgrace would have motivated the women to do everything in their power to conceal what happened to Lucretzia's daughter, Elena, on the night of June 27. Investigators were presented with a bargaining chip to offer a mother desperate to preserve her daughter's safety, honor, and marriage prospects.

Though agents may have harbored suspicions or even had in hand information confirming that Elena had been raped or sold, they had no compelling interest in publicly disclosing the girl's violation. A conspiracy of silence shielding Elena Lucretzia just fine from the investigator's point of view. Till and McMurray could be hanged only once, and conviction on charges of murdering one woman plus raping two others would do the trick. Why drag in poor Elena. Why put a child through the ordeal of testifying to her shame. We certainly won't, not if you say exactly what we tell you to say, Signora Lucretzia. Repeat what we tell you to say and we'll hang those black bastards. She's nodding, yes. *Yes, yes . . . Sì, sì.* Cooperate with us, signora, the agent continues, and we won't mention Elena's name during court-martial. Help us and we promise to guard your daughter's reputation.

Seventy years after the facts of murder and mayhem, what kinds of rules should govern my reconstruction of events that transpired the night of June 27–28 in Civitavecchia. Unless I offer an open-and-shut case to contradict the official record, won't I be imitating Louis Till. Wind up like Till. Swinging in the breeze. An irrelevancy. Bearing witness to alternative scenarios I'm able to render only as unspeakable absences. The inside of Till's mind an echo chamber of questions no one asks. Over and over Till hears questions not asked. How can he respond to questions nobody's asking. Except with silence to match silenced questions.

I can't rescue dead Louis Till from prison and the hangman. The Till file's my hobbyhorse. Me astride it like some kind of chocolate Don Quixote. I can't save Till. Not father, not son. Too late for the Tills. Louis Till's case is colder than Rakhim's. Why not work for live prisoners, my wife has asked me. Millions of people are locked up this very minute. *I do. I am*, I want to say. Want to explain to her, to myself. I work for an incarcerated son and brother. They are locked inside me, I am imprisoned with them during every moment that I struggle with the Till file. No choice. Trying to find words to help them. To help myself. Help carry the weight of hard years spent behind bars. If I return to Till's grave, I will confess to him first thing that the Louis Till project is about saving a son and brother, about saving myself.

Lying awake in the cottage near the gulf, I stared into darkness and wondered where the very deepest part of the deep blue sea would be. *Mer*, the French word for sea, sounds like the French word for mother. If the words for sea and mother sounded alike in English, would I be closer to having a mother now, I asked myself, then tried to think about nothing in particular, waited for the sweet oblivion of sleep, and that's when I heard the sea, its sound part of the room's silence all along, nonstop inside me, forgotten or not, it doesn't forget, it's there like my mother's there, speaking to me always. She's where I come from, where I belong, we belong to each other, and I will return. I can't help it. There's no other way. I go there in memories and will go there in whatever form memories assume once consciousness ends. I listen and remember her like the sea is remembered by shapes, substances strewn on the sand. By wind that sows and chases smells of the sea. By uncountable things and fragments of things brittle, soft, almost water, almost stone that feed, swim, watch noisy or silent as I watch and listen. I see myself in shells, rocks, strands of seaweed, myself broken, whole, see her, see us letting go and not letting go, and I understand no more than that. Many, many separations and returns shrouded in darkness, deep blue-black darkness of night that contains the sea, frees the sea, hides the sea. The sea far away though it's close. Inside me like my mother now, invisible, seachanged. As close as I'm ever going to get to having her.

War stories. Sea stories. Love stories. Till file full of stories. Of lies and truth. Shake them up. Dump them on the table. Then what. Why. Louis Till not stuck like a bone in the country's throat. America's forgotten Louis Till, no sweat. It's me. I'm the one who can't forget. My wars. My loves. My fear of violent death. I'm afraid Louis Till might be inside me. Afraid that someone looking for Louis Till is coming to pry me apart.

Selfish. Just like him. Just like your father. Mean and selfish like him and not a soul in the world you care about besides yourself, my mother shouted, her face close enough to mine to touch.

I can't recall exactly how old I was—suddenly conscious of being taller than her so I must have been in my early teens—but I will never forget my mother's words: *selfish. Just like him.* Words I heard more than once afterwards, and whether she truly believed them or wanted to shame me and save me from becoming the person the words described, whether she believed I was that selfish person then and still him the very last day I touched her flesh on this earth, I can't say. She's wherever she is and I am here, who I am. Still stung, still recoiling from her words. Wedded to the words for better or worse as she was wedded to my father, the man she loved who deserted her and their five children, the oldest of whom I am. First born, bearer of my father's name and, according to my mother, bearer of his intense, boundless self-love that admits no space to love another. Bearer of his willed blindness and hard, ice-cold capacity to separate himself from the lives of others as if other lives don't exist or don't matter. Or matter only because of what he could take from them, what they might willingly surrender.

Since I envisioned my father as almost a god in my mother's eyes, it's strange I heard only repudiation and scorn in her words. *Just like him.* No hint of redeeming resemblances, no backhanded compliment or unintended praise. My father exacted unconditional love and acceptance from my mother. Love that survived his fairly regular disappearances, disloyalties, his contemptuous manner of ignoring her, turning his back and walking away from her good sense, patience, her pleas, tears, the aching need for him in her voice. I believed her bottomless love granted him immunity from the consequences of his selfishness. No sweet immunity for me. The day she accused me of being like him, her words didn't condemn my father, they condemned me. My fatal flaw. Flawed like him but without the saving grace of being him. Her words orphaned me, separated me from her, my father, my siblings. All decent people.

I was too young then to comprehend very much about what held my parents together or what caused trouble between them. Too much love, no love, stupid love. My father seemed unhurtable and always in control so I blamed him for my parents' troubles. Stayed angry at him. Especially when he made my mother cry. Ashamed I couldn't defend her. All the while, in my most secret places, I envied, coveted my father's power.

Mostly, of course, I was jealous. Inconsolably so. As only a colored first son can be. Beyond reason. Acutely, unflaggingly aware when my father was at the center of my mother's attention. There was a different quality in how she tended to the rest of us if my father was around. She'd wear herself out as usual doing anything and everything for her kids, far beyond the call of duty, providing the necessities plus extras we whined for and expected, selfish extras spoiling us my father would grumble. But managing five demanding kids was never enough to complete my mother's day. She would plop down finally in her favorite kitchen chair and shoo us to bed or homework, impatient for us to be out of the way so a portion of her day we could not beg, steal, or borrow, could begin. If my father didn't come home, that portion empty. Her eyes expectant and worried. Fragile. But no matter how exhausted, how wilted she appeared or how weak her voice, I knew she'd revive if my father made it back.

I was a spy. Studied my mom's moods, actions. Believed I could eavesdrop on her thoughts. Registered each time she squandered on one of my siblings a juicy morsel of food, a smile, a kind word which should have been saved for me, the eldest son. Worse, much worse when she lavished a special attention on my father. My favorite moment of any day—him leaving. Door slammed shut behind him. *Going out,* his phrase to cover any destination—work, Henderson's Barbershop to play a number, crosstown to drink with his cronies. Ten minutes, ten hours, a whole day or night—whatever. *Going out.* My mother knew better than to ask what *out* meant. Knew better than to rile him by asking where or how long. She seldom risked challenging his silence because she might find out more than she was able to handle if his mood happened to be brutal honesty.

Selfish. Just like him. When she addressed those words to me, my mother acknowledged the vulnerable place inside herself where my father reigned absolutely. Unopposed, unopposable, my view back then, because he didn't care. To have her or lose her—neither mattered to him. He didn't give a good goddamn push come to shove, about her or anyone else. Didn't care. Wore his not caring like armor. No one, nothing could touch him. Change him. What my mother shouted at me one day wasn't news to her or me. Both of us had understood for a long while that I possessed the power to hurt her. Listening closer then and now I hear more disappointment than anger or scorn in my mother's voice. *Just like him.* Too late for me to refuse the legacy bequeathed father to son. His meager and overwhelming gift. The chilling distance I feared in him. Distance that isolated, exiled me. Empowered me to hurt those who love me.

The day my mother accused me of being *Just like him,* I understood *him* to be my father. Half a century or so later, *him* not so easy to pin down. I paid only superficial attention back then to the *Him* my mother addressed as her Heavenly Father. Knew nothing yet about Louis Till or his doomed son my age, Emmett. My mother had not heard the name Till either. Nevertheless, she grew up a kind of sister to Mamie Till, accommodated herself to the same unnerving fact that Mamie Tills of the world confront. A disturbingly simple fact: every time a *him,* a colored male person they love, man or boy, leaves and the door shuts behind him, door to a dwelling in which they are attempting to make something of their lives together, there's a good chance that he, *him*, that colored male person, won't return. Not when she expects anyway. Or needs him most. Maybe not ever. Once he leaves the space they are struggling to secure for their mutual benefit, for the benefit maybe of their children, once *he's* beyond the door and out in a world which does not love him, there are no guarantees. Except shit will cross his path. Deep shit that won't make it easy or simple for a colored *him* to come back clean, in one piece. A miracle if for years he's able to go out and come back regularly from a steady job and still be more or less alive. No miracles operate to return him unchanged. Changed far too often for the worse by a world that refuses to welcome him. Or worse. Very much worse. A world acknowledging his presence only as chaos. Denying his name, his dignity. To stay alive he becomes very, very selfish. Very silent. As if nothing can touch him or hurt him or ever will.

Hardness and selfishness a means of survival once *he* steps out the door. *Out.* The survival rule for women like my mother and Mamie Till is they must adjust. They must change, too, or be destroyed. Fathers, sons, brothers, husbands, lovers, if they survive, return changed. A wife or mother learns to be grateful if her *him* doesn't disappear altogether or die in spirit before he's dead. Often the man or boy who returns is a silent stranger, hard and selfish, little or no resemblance to the special one she had hoped for, prayed for, bargained for, dreamed of when she offered *him* some or all her love. Love no doubt she should have known better than to risk, given all the terrible stories, sermons, songs, gossip, hearts broken, women with features frozen into masks of bitterness or emptiness or just plain pitiful looking. And often she does know better, but gives, despite knowing better, some or all her love.

My mother shared with Mrs. Till certain unyielding truths about their men, about *him,* father son husband, holy ghost. Truths my mother feared in me. Truths leading to this admonition: no point moaning and begging, weeping and wailing when he, when your *him* says he's going out the door and you're afraid maybe he never will return and you start carrying on like you don't have good sense—stop your foolishness. Where else is he supposed to go if not *out.* If he believes he's a man, he's going out. And do what he has to do to survive. Do his dirt. His selfish things. Going, going, gone. Leaving you alone inside four walls. Alone with your unrequited or doomed or vanished or imaginary or lost or punished love. Alone to chew on your fingernails, chew on your love. Unless you change, too.

Not nice. My mother said the night she caught me looking. I'm still ashamed she had to say the words aloud to me—*not nice.* I knew better. Deep down inside myself I knew better and had worked diligently to teach myself to look away from my mother if the close quarters of the small apartment into which she was crammed with a husband and five kids exposed her half-dressed or naked body to my gaze. From the moment I understood I was a boy, her son, a male, and she was a female, a woman as well as my mother, I treated her body as a site of certain privacies I could not and should not share. I understood my eyes could trespass and hurt her. Make her sad. Sadden myself because looking put something I couldn't cope with in my hands, in my mind. Mixed up my mother's body and mine. My shame and privacy mixed up with hers. Far too much for a boy to deal with. So I just didn't look. Looked away. From a certain age on, I knew better, always averted my eyes. Feeling each time a warm flush of warning that strangely came after instead of before the look I avoided.

I believed I had tamed my curiosity about what I shouldn't see. Until once. Then there I was. On my knees in the dark hallway outside the downstairs bathroom we shared with the Lemingtons. Drawn by the quiet of the absent Lemingtons away visiting relatives in Georgia. Drawn by familiar noises, louder in the end of day stillness. Water running, my mother's body sloshing in the tub, faucets on and off, a roar in the pipes, then creaking until silence returns after each blast of water. Drawn to the steps by a pinprick of light on the landing below, I tipped down. Dropped to one knee in the dark hallway to see the bright world on the other side of the door. Not to spy on my mother. To spy on a woman's naked body, courtesy of my mother, if I knelt and peered through the keyhole.

A confusion of shapes and colors appeared and before I could make conclusive sense of anything—of what was only inches away, moving inside the bathroom—my mother's voice came from the other side of the door, *that's not a nice thing to do.* Then a washcloth or towel draped over the end of a doorknob killed the light that peeked through the keyhole. An unfortunate once, and neither my mother nor I ever spoke about it all the years after. One of our secrets. Her words through the door said perhaps everything that needed to be said. Her words and silence that followed. What could I possibly say in response. Her words branded me forever the instant I heard them. Red letters across my guilty forehead. *Selfish. Just like him.* I'm sorry. So sorry. I'll never do the not nice thing again. Unspoken words a boy, a man, a *him* might have said aloud to stop the burning but didn't. I'm sorry. Forgive me, please.

I got lucky with weather during my stay in Brittany. Even on the one morning when rain apparently imminent and I decided that to avoid getting soaked, I better jog not walk my usual route. Somewhere near the run's midpoint, I revved up my pace. Glory surge toward an imaginary halfway finished line until heat in my chest and lead in my legs forced me to slow down. No bargaining. End of discussion. Click. Lights out.

I dropped to the sand, flat on my back, legs splayed. Above me faint slashes of blue here and there but the sky was still overcast—vast expanses of dull, featureless gray, a few rippled banks of clouds the dirty color of old snow piled on city streets. Good burn in my thighs and also a warning they need a rest if I expect them to repeat the distance they'd just humped. I pulled off the red bandanna knotted do-rag style round my head, wrung it dry as I could, and wiped salty streaks from my sunglasses, mopped sweat from my face.

Nothing much to see in the deserted cove except sky and sea, presences too large to miss, clean glasses or not. The gray weight of sky. Gray roar of water. At the cove's far bend white eruptions of foam exploded above giant black boulders. Was the tide receding or creeping back, millimeter by millimeter, to cover flat stretches of sand studded with rocks it had uncovered earlier. If I returned to this spot in an hour, would it be submerged. Water always moving, one tide subdued and subduing the next, but my eyes were unable to detect the tide's direction. Wind beating into my face becomes visible as I watch gulls soar, dive, glide, skim the shallows for prey, white wing tips blinking in the grayness of sky and sea.

About a hundred yards away in one of the miniature pools formed within clumps of rocks along the shore, a tall white bird high-steps, long legs thin as threads, beak a needle. It appears more intent on elegance than fishing as it struts slow motion, pin head bobbing atop elastic stem of neck. The bird's awkward medley of parts plays a kind of syncopated rhythm, repeating the same routine to execute each short stride—weight balanced on one stick leg while the other leg lifted slowly, cautiously, breaking at an invisible knee, the two parts of it hinged at a right angle, a long foot dangling, suspended above the shallow pool, then slowly replanted until the leg ramrod straight again in the sea, waiting for the other leg to organize the next lazy, mini step. Meanwhile, the spear of beak darts into the pool every now and then, an off-time beat punctuating the nonchalant stroll. For whom was this bird on double-jointed stilts performing. Fastidious, careful locomotion, more saunter, more ghetto bop than wading in water. Is it concerned about the state of its feet. Raising them for inspection, making sure long toes and hooked talons are not sullied with mud.

When it flutters up, out of water into air, *up* a stuttering rise, a matter of stages that slow time again like its high-stepping strut through water. The bird hovers until its wings, four, maybe five feet tip to tip, catch sufficient wind under them, then it veers sharply out to sea. In full flight it becomes a black silhouette circling higher and higher. Swift, imperial, on its breast a swastika emblazoned in a crimson crest, a bundle of lightning bolts in one claw. Louis Till gripped in the other.

A Nazi war eagle in Brittany's gray sky. But Nazis didn't hang Louis Till, did they. Till had more to fear from his own army than from Hitler's legions. Nazi Germany did not invent war or race or genocide. Many wars waged before and after World War II. Wars being waged today whose purpose is to eliminate entire so-called races of people. Us. My people. Done to us. Done to others. Done by us. Done to each other. I was drifting.

Drifting. Hiding. Going nowhere. Somewhere beside an ocean I'd flown across just days before. Nicely exhausted, nicely sprawled on the sand a few days after finding Louis Till's grave. Daydreaming evil birds. Soon I would revisit Plot E or not. Return to the States, and still nowhere. Still adrift. No closer, no clearer. Closer to what. Clearer about what.

The sky was still threatening, but no rain yet. I decided to walk not jog back to the cottage Antoine's grandfather had purchased. I think I would have welcomed a drenching rain as I returned along the wooded coastline broken by small and large inlets, estuaries, coves, bays, channels the tide fills and empties predictably so during certain hours you can swim in brisk salt water, other times of day the same stretch a sea of mud. If I had not reversed direction after my stop, in an hour or so I would have reached Vannes, the Gulf of Morbihan's center of commerce and tourism whose prosperous citizens had once commissioned stained glass church windows from artists like Antoine's grandfather, the grandfather from whom he inherited the secrets of *pâte de verre,* a technique for coloring and molding glass. Vannes, where in 1731 the great-great-grandfathers of today's citizens had pooled money to outfit a ship, the *Diligent,* for a voyage from Vannes to ports in West Africa where slaves could be purchased cheaply then sold in Martinique for enormous profit.

In Paris Antoine had shown me slides of his new work on exhibit in Nice. Transparent cubes, globes, chunks of glass with all sorts of unpredictable things displayed inside—antique coins, pressed flowers, perfect miniaturized replicas of frogs, lizards, snakes, seams of color, Latin and Greek inscriptions, a cluster of grapes—things which seemed to both swim and be frozen, trapped and liberated within glass walls. I'd always been intrigued by my friend's work, its roots in ancient Egypt, necromancy, alchemy, and family tradition. The best of the new pieces continued an investigation of time, his whispered conversation with time I could eavesdrop upon. Time engaged. Time a medium both intimate and distant. A medium transparent and opaque as glass. All life sealed in glass and glass itself sealed within a sheath of uncertainties that allow it to assume forms as various as fire, water, air, earth. Glass complicit with time yet not quite able to alter or evade it. Lives encased in glass doomed to repeat and suffer history. Bearing witness again and again to time's unchangeable grip.

* * *

In the shuffle of Paris slides one in particular had caught my attention. An ebony-tinted block about twenty by twenty-four inches, five inches deep, containing thousands of tiny bubbles like breath bubbles or stars trapped in the implausible vastness of its interior, a galaxy of stars along with one immense bubble, a bone white, see-through sphere filling nearly a third of the sculpture's actual volume. A dark, purplish spill spreads down the sphere. Letters from a foreign alphabet are visible in neat black rows through the purple cloud. The letters glow mysteriously and though they seem solid, substantial, they also crackle or dance or shiver bearing the weight of many, many indecipherable messages. The piece unsettled me like those darkly uncertain shapes of roadkill when I walk or jog.

Roadkill is always my first reaction when I notice some unrecognizable dark form lying up ahead alongside my path. Something randomly, violently emptied of life, I think, though obviously I'm not sure what it is, nor sure how or when or even if death struck it, or what kind of death, and not exactly sure I want to know either.

Dead how long. A grisly, lumpish body part or remains of an entire creature. I won't know until I get closer and sometimes uncertain even when I reach whatever it is lying there and halfway inspect it or halfway ignore it or a little bit of both usually while I pass. Often, I will keep guessing, wondering after the shape's long gone behind me. Alive once. Dead once. Alive again as I had glimpsed it up ahead. Now dead again. Alive or dead perhaps not separate. Not either/or. A matter of time. Of now you see it, now you don't.

* * *

In an essay started the second night in the cottage, I had attempted to figure out at last, at last, what it was about those shapes beside the road that compelled me to look and look away, look at them and through them. Why do they seem like windows and mirrors. What connects them to ideas about mortality and time embodied in Antoine's *pâte de verre* sculptures. I didn't get very far with the essay. The dark shapes ambushed and eluded me as they did when I encountered them on a road. Words I squeezed out in the cottage could not express how the dark shapes beckoned sometimes like a yawning grave. I blamed the essay's failure that night on too much head, not enough heart, on thinking instead of feeling my way into a subject. Then next day, the overcast day of running and walking along the Gulf of Morbihan, I blamed heart. Heart too full of things I wasn't prepared to deal with, including ungenerous envy of any art's success while my Louis Till project falters. Heart stymied. Head unable to craft words that did more than register confusion, report uneasiness and sadness. Head. Heart. Dark somethings alive and dead along a highway. No explanations. Heart. Head. Failure can't be explained. No more than Louis Till's birth or his son, Emmett's death. Or a sculpture, a novel, a painting, a song. Equally mysterious and banal. Mortal. We try and fail. To fail is to fail is to fail.

The Till project has stalled. I'm adrift. Probably on purpose. Probably conscious flight. Running. Hiding. As if I can close the distance between whatever it is I possess and what I've lost. Running. Hiding. South to collect villains and family stories. France to find a grave, jellyfish, a dead uncle's shoes, talking stones, glass sculptures. Nowhere to put it all, no way to connect, bind together scattered bits and pieces. To render them lifelike, usable, or even better, free them from darkness that surrounds and consumes. Free the power of those gleanings, details, remains. Fragments shored against ruin as a poet friend of the imprisoned poet called them. Do words have power to create more life. To reach back far enough or forward enough and help me enter Louis Till's silence. Mine. Words on these pages. My file, my story. These words I chase to represent a life. Who will open the file. Read the words. What will they make of me, us, after I'm silenced, like you, Louis Till.

On that gray day, I needed to let words go, but could not. Figured the next best thing might be to pretend I could. I decided—as I decide far too often when I feel control slipping away—to deny heart, head. Shut them down. Concentrate on walking, the simple physical effort of following one footstep with another. Summoned all the good music I knew to play and play and play while I made my way back to the cottage.

Images from a Paris slide show vanished. One sudden, short blaze of sunshine parted densely packed layers of cloud, then they zippered shut for good. No light overhead, but heaps and strands of algae like shadows littering the sand. Like people's hair on a barbershop floor. People's butchered hair stolen, stored in a warehouse in a scene from a grainy documentary that had popped up one night in New York City on the History channel. Blues and gospel, gospel and blues, rhythm and blues inside my head stopped abruptly and I found myself silently counting with each step the number of dead it would take to produce mounds and swarms and hills of hair. Human hair in a warehouse, hair the color of tangles of seaweed strewn on the beach.

I had instructed myself to walk away from things I couldn't bear to see and things I couldn't say, but my count, my steps on an overcast afternoon in Brittany mourned the dead. Mourned each lost person's lost name. Names borne once, alive once, spoken once. Unspeakable now. Names only the sea remembers like it remembers to keep track of the ebb and flow of tides. Remembering, counting. Infinitely patient and precise. The way Clement from the barbershop remembered every number bet. Who won. Who lost. How many pennies, dimes, quarters, dollars wagered. Remembering, counting. How many dead are required to fashion trails, pools, streams of dark algae on the sand, how many heads shorn naked to produce a bale of clipped hair, how many fistfuls of hair to pack bale after bale. Hair curled, braided, twisted, spooled. Silent bales stacked to reach the ceilings of vast rooms.

No mother's voice for company that afternoon. No one speaking. My mother's face a pale mask. Lips painted too pink, closed eyelids sealed too tightly by grains of powder. Faces of my dead father and brother, grandfathers and grandmothers, the lost smile of my imprisoned brother's lost son, the smile of the baby girl my sister lost. The dead face I had imagined for Clement. His own ghost name he never spoke. His limp, when I first saw him from my grandfather's shoulders. His broom guiding quiet, quiet hair across the barbershop floor. Emptiness opened under my feet and I plummeted within a medium not quite silence, not hair, more like the sea's moan no one notices most of the time because it's always there.

* * *

Step inside Henderson's Barbershop Saturday, late afternoon, and Clement or no Clement, you can't help stepping on hair. Hair everywhere. And voices. Chairs have been full of customers since eight a.m. Some men hang out all day long. Father and son march in for the son's first cut. A boy, first time solo in a barber chair, looks around to see who's looking. Boosters duck in and out many times on Saturday to sell fabulous shit they steal. Colored janitors, lawyers, garbagemen, clerks, laborers, a dentist, a cop. Talk, talk, talking. Colored men of all colors. Men in work coveralls. Men Saturday night sharp at noon. A show when I'm a youngblood in a barber chair or waiting my turn seated below mirrors that double, triple the Saturday action inside Henderson's.

I wanted to be one of the dudes bopping in from big cars, sporting the perforated leather, two-tone Stacy Adams shoes Big Jim wore and everybody wished they could afford. Some men quiet as Clement, others tell loud stories that begin in the middle and never end, play on and on like serials at the Belmar show where my grandmother or an aunt used to drop me off Saturday morning to join the line of other little colored kids, hot dime in our fists, hungry for a day of Technicolor double features cartoons, an action-packed, black and white *serial.*

The word *serial* was a puzzle the first time I heard it. *Cereal,* what we ate with milk and sugar in bowls at breakfast, right. No. Same sound *serial* also a story, my aunt Geraldine explained. Same tale that's a different tale each time, I finally figured out. Like one Saturday morning you'd see a pretty white lady tied up on the train tracks and a big black locomotive snorting down the rails to run her over. *Better git out the way, fool.* Engine gets bigger and bigger. Fills the screen. Lady screams. Every little kid in the Belmar screams. Steam whistle shrieks. Steel wheels cut up the poor, soft, pretty, tied-up lady. *Told you git out the way, didn't I.* But the screen goes black so you miss the chance to see her bloody, chopped up bones and meat. *TO BE CONTINUED.* Then you pay your dime next Saturday morning and she ain't even dead at all. Huh-uh. Cowboy fool in a big white hat snatches her off the tracks. She's safe as a sack of potatoes curled up in his arms. Lady gone so the hooting train runs over nobody. Some kids clap and whoop and dance in their seats. Big *BOOOO* when the pretty lady hugs the cowboy's neck, kisses his cheek. Serials don't worry about last time, just this time, just keep on running Saturday after Saturday. Like same barbershop story always a different story. Serials remember only what they want to remember, but who cares long as it's a good lie.

Louis Till's story is a serial. *To be continued* glows in white letters each time the screen darkens. The word *Clement* starts it again. Clement who drools, limps, Clement who never speaks, never ages. Who doesn't turn up one day in Henderson's and nobody says, Clement dead. They say *Clement tired of youall's foolishness. Gone to sweep out another barbershop.* But I knew better. Even as a boy I had known Clement was dead and could take me away, turn me dead like him. Clement's red rag caked with blood and his nasty, dead filth. Frankenstein-Dracula–Wolf Man face of Clement in the mirror spins into my dreams. There's spooky silence in the name *Clement.* In the huge boot his foot drags. No one ever hears Clement speak his own name and after he's gone who would want to hear him say it. First time I saw him in the Homewood streets I knew he was a ghost and from that moment on I was sure he would sneak up one day and *Boo.* Holler his name in my ear. Steal my life.

Clement. Horse-faced, parchment yellowish Clement who never spoke and seemed not to age during my decades of haircuts in Henderson's Barbershop. Mr. Henderson dead, his three sons, my peers, grown up to be barbers like their daddy, and Tito, one of them who used to cut my hair, dead like his father and my father, and Clement still sweeping balls of hair off Henderson's floor. Clement's never a day older. His jaw hangs wide open while he sweeps, polishes, tidies up, scrubs, mops, hobbles out on errands, plays people's numbers in the tobacco shop up the Avenue. Say a number once to Clement, he never forgets it. If you're a player, say your figure to Clement because his head count is truer than numbers scratched on slips of paper. Clement's the final judge. When disagreements grow too loud, everybody's paid off or loses according to the numbers Clement speaks with his fingers. Clement's always busy, busy, except once in a while on the hottest days he catnaps on an upturned milk crate beside the window whose large red letters spell out *Henderson Barber Shop,* letters which also could have said *Clement Orphan Shop.* He sits on his crate like he owns the whole wide world. Says not a word, looks not a minute older year after year. Just fewer and fewer teeth, more stumps, snags, gaps.

Just before Mr. Henderson died and his surviving sons took over the shop, he bought Clement a shiny, new grill of white teeth. Clement wore them, but still drooled, losing spit and sneezing sprays of spit just like the first time my father sat me in Mr. Henderson's chair and Mr. Henderson skinned my head and I couldn't take my eyes off the yellow boy or small yellow man who pushed a push broom up and back, back and up. Mr. Henderson hollered, *Boy, wipe your mouth,* at the horse-faced yellow boy or little yellow man who pulls a nasty rag from his back pocket, mops his long chin.

The nasty red snot rag in Clement's hand had made me shudder, almost made me sick. I was close to throwing up, already close to tears that first time in a barber's chair because my father was mad at me and Mr. Henderson's electric clippers lawn-mowing every last blade of my nice, thick, nappy hair, hair uncut till that morning. Boo-hoo, what's happened to all my nice hair. Hair the women at home loved to pat and comb and brush and *coo-coo.* They'd tuck me under my chubby chin, *coo-coo*, or pinch my dimples, *pretty hair, look at hims pretty long hair, ain't him a handsome boy, sweet boy.*

Clement in my dreams for years. Since the first time I saw him. His two big nose holes. Two big eye holes red moons inside a yellowish sky. Clement's spitty mouth never closed, never said a word. Was he sorry for me or teasing me, first time I sat in a barber chair. Did Clement catch me spying on him or was he spying peekaboo on me while I searched for myself and couldn't find myself in the wraparound wall mirrors that mashed together, pulled apart everything in Henderson's.

Clement memories jump-start many stories. Talked stories that flow, merge into the name Clement never speaks. Clement's quiet broom pushing balls of hair unheard unless Henderson's empty and if Henderson's empty who would hear except Clement. Ghost silence of everybody's hair, same, same on the floor, gone off the top of whomever's head it once covered, heads shaved cue ball bare, same, same. Soundlessness of clumps of hair dropping on the floor, a mound of hair or many mounds, same, same, pushed slowly together, mounds growing wider, deeper.

Deeper than the deep blue sea is what I thought, a kid once upon a time, first time, first haircut in Mr. Henderson's chair, stomach knotted, bare feet sinking deeper and deeper into wormy masses of swarming, clammy hair. Close to tears. Lips quivering. Afraid I'd lose control altogether and blubber if I tried to open my mouth to answer my father. *What in hell's wrong with you, boy.* My father definitely not happy with me. Ashamed of me. Ashamed for me because I was acting silly in public. Behaving like a sissy first time in a barber chair. Disappointment fills my father's eyes. He tries to shake off his own shame and embarrassment. Nods *tsk, tsk,* at Mr. Henderson. But I couldn't help it. Couldn't stop. I sniffed, trembled in the cavernous chair. Sank deeper and deeper into its soft cushions. Drowning. Eyes, ears, mouth, nose slowly sucked down through layers of slime. Smelled it, tasted it. Blinded by thick, wiggling yards and miles of people's silent hair. People's sheared off, dead hair like ropes and piles of algae, it could have been algae, endless mile after mile of dark sea waste I envisioned, though at that age I had not been near the ocean, knew nothing about seaweed I'd see one afternoon in Brittany imitating stolen hair.

On my second day in France, Antoine had driven me from Paris to Oise-Aisne to search for Louis Till's grave. We parked across the road from the imposing stone portals of the main cemetery, in a lot next to an administrative building with nobody at home around noon when we arrived, so after a brief browse unescorted through two small rooms of artifacts and photos that illustrate the history of the American Cemetery and Memorial, we exited a rear door, same door probably Alice Kaplan had exited in 2004, but we had no administrator to guide us. We walked about a hundred yards in the wrong direction towards a combination garage and utility shed beside which some workers were finishing lunch, others loading equipment on vehicles, a crew of groundskeepers in gray-striped coveralls who nodded, *no, huh-uh,* or dropped their eyes when I asked in my best French about the location of Plot E, until one of them, pale blue eyes shaded by a Phillies baseball cap, pointed across the road in the direction of the vast cemetery proper where the person might be who could answer questions about a smaller, separate burial site. Given the workers' not unfriendly though guarded responses, I didn't want to cross the road just yet because any official who could help could also be a pain-in-the-ass and order us to go away.

We waited until all the workers walked or drove off, then poked around in sparse woods below the shed and garage, me gradually realizing as we checked out the terrain that I had no idea how distant or disguised a graveyard for dishonored dead I had read about in a book might be if its custodians wished to conceal its presence. After we had circled through the trees and wound up more or less back where we'd entered them, we mounted a slight slope that leveled off not far beyond the administrative building, and at the top of the rise, confronted by a high, thick mass of trees and shrubbery, we hesitated again, not wishing to be caught skulking around, not quite ready to abandon the search either, unsure what to do next, until one of us decided to push aside some branches, slip inside a small break in the dense barrier of greenery to see what might lie beyond it. One, two, three cautious steps, ducking, bobbing, weaving to avoid thorny branches, and there we were inside a circle of pines and laurel at the edge of a serenely green, set-aside space that contained one small, freestanding stone cross and ninety-six identical, four-by-four-inch, flat white stones arranged in parallel rows, each stone bearing a number just as Alice Kaplan's book, *The Interpreter,* had informed readers they would.

Beneath each white marker embedded in the slightly sloping, meticulously groomed lawn, if Kaplan and numerous other sources I'd consulted were accurate, lay the remains of dishonored American soldiers who had been executed by the U.S. Army during World War II and transported here for reinterment sometime around 1949 from burial grounds in various countries that once constituted the Mediterranean and European *theaters,* so to speak, of World War II.

Louis Till's grave, *The Interpreter* said, is number 73, to our right, at the near corner of Plot E's rectangular arrangement of four rows, twenty-four graves per row.

Till's grave is exactly like all the others. Marked by a small flat stone with probably an underground zinc liner beneath it containing a wooden box containing another wood box containing remains. Eighty-three of the ninety-six graves hold colored remains. Each of the ninety-six is allotted approximately half the room allotted to each of the 6,012 graves for honored dead across the road, graves for casualties of a battle fought nearby, one of the fiercest of World War I. In the official American Cemetery and Memorial of Oise-Aisne, a thirty-five-acre expanse constituted of Plots A through D, the headstones of the honored dead are tall crosses of white marble, imported from Carrara, Italy, crosses deployed so that, *as one proceeds through the cemetery, their long rows rise gently from the main entrance . . . presenting an ever changing array of geometric patterns.*

Inside Plot E, I had stepped away from Antoine to be alone. Moved closer to Louis Till's marker, close enough to speak privately to Louis Till on this, our first meeting, this first chance to say hello, goodbye, whatever. A silent exchange, of course. Like silence within glass sculptures. Like silence Antoine and I had maintained since entering Plot E, as if a sign forbidding talk on pain of death had been posted beside the gap we found through the thicket of greenery enclosing the dishonored graves.

No conversation with Antoine. None with Louis Till, either. I could not pretend Louis Till would hear a greeting, a benediction spoken or unspoken. Nor pretend Till's silence signified anything other than Till's absence.

No Louis Till. No man under marker 73. Full-size, grown men laid out properly on their backs would not fit into the cramped spaces defined by Plot E's grid of stones. Then what the fuck was under each marker. Inside a zinc liner, inside wooden boxes. What did the army find in 1949 when they dug up and pried open the original coffin containing Louis Till's remains. A uniformed or naked corpse folded up like a fetus. A skeleton wearing rags of flesh. Heap of dust, hair, teeth. Trash bag of ashes. Remains. What remained. Did they chop Till up, break his bones to fit into a container designed for Plot E's stingy dimensions. After you tie a man's hands, blindfold him, put a noose around his neck, drop him through a trapdoor, let him swing in the breeze, shitting and pissing on himself, neck broken, heart stopped, was it possible to inflict more injury, more insult and dishonor on his body. On his remains. Who conceived the idea to exhume the dishonorable dead and reinter them in this isolated, separate, restricted Plot E. Who conceived the elaborate specifications and protocols of the reburial project. Who contracted mortuary specialists to execute the plan.

I wanted to rip Till's plaque out of the ground. Hurl it far away. A scream, growl, curse, moan, howl wanted to leap from my throat. Something, anything to disrupt Plot E's preposterous dignity. Why the obscenity, the madness, the irony of special handling, costly attention devoted to a man after he's been reduced to dead meat. Rotting meat and bones exhumed, then trucked, shipped, riding a train, flying through the air to wind up in hole number 73, one of ninety-six four-by-four holes more appropriate in size for burying large dogs than men.

If you stood beside Louis Till's grave today what would you hear. Probably not the cries I kept inside myself. Would you hear blood. Blood's loud flow a river dividing humankind. Blood of crimes in Italy. Crimes in Mississippi. Blood deep. Blood guilt. Till blood. Evidence loud and clear in the stillness of Plot E. The Till father condemned by dark blood at birth. An orphan no one claims. Origins unknown. Probably not quite human. A beast to be penned, tamed, worked, slaughtered. The son's fate differs only slightly. False innocence his crime. Blood chose Emmett Till. His time was cut short to demonstrate what bright blood must be willing to do if it wishes brightness to live on and on. To thrive and prosper uncorrupted.

Louis Till's story, his son Emmett's, mine, my father's, my family's could begin or end there. With a story of stolen sugar. With a blood price exacted for theft. With rage. With resignation. With grief. Mourning. With ancient bloody lies twisting inside me. A scream I suppressed. Silent screams of the dishonored dead filed in boxes at my feet. Lost names. Lost faces.

My visit to the dishonored graves didn't last long. I forced myself to look away from Louis Till's numbered stone. Stared at pine trees and laurel bushes that had been planted to shield Plot E from view. The perimeter of bushes and trees had grown quite tall. Evidently it was no one's job to trim the top of it, blackly green and sprawling scraggly against clear blue sky. I could pick out individual branches, twigs, thorns, briars high above Plot E's neat lawn. I kept my eyes fixed up there until I began to feel the dark barrier circling, closing behind my back. I traced the entire circle in my mind one more time. What I could see of it, what I could not see. I followed it again, one last time even more slowly, slowly, then lowered my eyes to find Antoine. Nodded at him and we walked back to his car.

The last morning in Brittany is hazy, a paleness which would steep to bright blue before noon. One final, long, leisurely walk felt like a good idea. No reason to hurry. No one waiting in the cottage for me to return. No last-minute chores. No place I needed to be until four when a taxi to the train station in Vannes was due. Then on to Paris, New York, home, my wife. A whole wide world out there, unchanged, imperturbable, unresolved whether I return or not. Return to a Till project or not. Louis Till's file no conundrum. It contained a simple story. Unresolved. Unchanged. Imperturbable.

During my walk that day I recalled something I'd never told a soul. A memory which had never formed itself into words. Not even words I'd said only inside my head. A secret *once,* once and only once, lost and buried as it happened. Silent as the silence surrounding it. Memory of the boy I had been when he found himself alone with Clement.

Inside the memory I was afraid. Past tears. Past hollering for help. Stranded alone with Clement while Clement finished his workday in Henderson's. Seeking a hiding place in what might or might not be a dream, I crouched in a shadowed corner of the barbershop. No doubt in my mind danger was real. Holding my breath, heart pounding, I hoped against hope Clement wouldn't catch me spying on him. I hid from him as I'd hide years later from a photo in *Jet* magazine of a colored boy's disfigured face, one eye swollen shut, the other eye missing. A dead, blind boy and no way to escape his awful, silent stare.

Clement peers into the mirror in Henderson's where I'd been watching him, and he is not the spooky Clement of my nightmares. He's a small, shy man. Our eyes meet. His finger taps his pursed lips, *Shhhh.* Then soundlessly his mouth forms the shape of his name, *Clement.* And *Clement* does not shatter quiet. Does not betray me.

In France beside his dishonored grave I had not spoken to Louis Till about Clement, about my father or mother, nor Latreesha, nor Promiseland. Nor about the statuette of Saint Martin de Porres, patron saint of the poor, the humble, of lost causes according to the elderly woman who took a shine to me and gave me a small wooden figurine as a farewell present in Chicago fifty-some years ago. Thomasina Hawks was her name, Tomahawk her street name, a fierce veteran of Chicago's deadly war on Black Panthers in the sixties. She was as full of stories as *Clement* was full of clamoring silences. Tommie gave me a talisman to keep me safe during my life's journey, she said.

* * *

I didn't tell Louis Till that for me it's always winter in Chicago. Windy city. Swirling snow and bitter, bitter cold. Unless it's a day warmed by Tommie's gift or September 1955, and I'm standing in the Twelfth Street Station, not too far from Mamie Till, waiting for the Emmett Till train. I didn't admit to Louis Till I'd lost the statuette of Saint Martin. Forgotten it for years until on the plane to France, leafing through an account of Pizarro's conquest of the Inca empire in Peru, I came across *Figure 10,* a photo of a contemporary votive card sold in front of Lima churches. *San Martin in the hospital infirmary with his trademark broom and one of his many miracles.*

Saint Martin de Porres, the book would inform me, renowned for piety, modesty, the all-forgiving leniency, mercy of his gaze, had spent most of his life as a lay brother, a nurse and domestic servant inside a Dominican monastery in Lima. He grew up in the turbulent sixteenth century, a period during which the Catholic Church was busy importing African slaves, slaughtering, converting, pacifying, enslaving Indians and *mestizos,* mixed people of color, like the Tills, me. Like Martin de Porres, illegitimate son of a Spanish knight and a Panamanian slave, his mother's African darkness effaced from the painted figurine Thomasina Hawks presented to me, but evident in the portrait of Porres as Saint Martin decorating the votive card. Same saint. My pale, lost wooden statuette and the colored San Martin pictured on the card in the book, broom in hand, his face a dark disk framed by a halo and at his feet the humble miracle of mouse, dog, cat, eating from one dish. Over his long-sleeved, snow-white alb he wears a flowing black cassock, gold cross on a chain draped from neck to knees. A white dove hovers at Saint Martin's right, and on his left, the sick with tiny crosses above their beds lie in an infirmary behind him.

* * *

In Plot E, since I had not yet discovered the fact, I couldn't tell Louis Till that in Brittany as I read further in Todorov's chronicle of Europe's ruthless subjugation of the Americas, I shook my head in good, old-fashioned wonder, startled, but also strangely unsurprised when I learned the father of Martin de Porres had apprenticed him to the trade of cutting hair and bloodletting and one of the boy's regular chores was to sweep the barbershop floor.

When I visit Louis Till again, I will try to find words to let him know Clement rescued me once, a secret once, from a boy's terror. Let him hear how I heard *Clement,* the silence of the name *Clement* echoing in the legend of a colored boy/man in Peru who swept day after day a barbershop floor, a monastery's stone paths. I must find ways to address Louis Till in the manner Louis Till speaks to me. Not only with words. Words are insufficient, much too late for only words. I must respect Till's absence. His silence. I must begin with doubled silences, absences. His. My own. Lost words, unspoken words. His. Mine. Begin with wishful thinking. With a language that exposes my naked hunger, the raw desire of my eyes to see, listen, speak, learn.

I will invent ways, Louis Till, to tell you Tommie Hawks bestowed a gift upon a young man, a gift she hoped would protect, guide, and light the long life she wished for him. Light that was hidden from you by a hood executioners dropped over your head, Louis Till. Extinguished in the photo of your murdered son Emmett's crushed dead face. Light I lose, forget, remember, dream. Found and lost, found again, lost again. Found in a stranger's eyes. In sad eyes, laughing eyes. It's always a great surprise and no surprise at all. Light I recall from my last day in Brittany, while I walked and listened deeper, longer to loneliness and darkness inside myself. Light in the watchful eyes of my people, living and dead just yesterday, and many, many years before. Luminous eyes I searched in the colored face of Saint Martin de Porres on a votive card reproduced in a book. The book I opened on a flight to find your grave in France.

Listen up, Saint Louis. I see you got one bubble eye half-open listening over there. Don't be falling asleep on us, man. Night's young. A lil corner left in the jug even though you bout drowned yourself trying to empty the motherfucker. Wake up, nigger. Don't start calling them hogs, boy. Loud as you snore it's a wonder you don't wake up your own damned self. Listen up, Till. You gonna like this story, my man. Read it in a book and Ima be nice and tell it to you cause everybody know you too ignorant to read shit your own self. Call it Fable of the Bees and the Bear in the book but I ain't telling it all. Just the part I know you'll like, Till, cause it's about these bees crazy as you. Kamikaze bees like them Jap Kamikaze planes they say tearing up Uncle Sam's navy over in the Pacific. What happens at the end of the story, see, is Brer Bear come fucking with a beehive looking for honey and all the bees gets riled up. Every damn mama bee, daddy bee, and every little jitterbug bee jump Brer Bear's burly ass. And while Brer Bear be swatting and growling and swinging his big self around every which a way inside a cloud of pissed-off bumblebees, some the wildest, meanest bees, them crazy Kamikaze motherfuckers, dives down the bear's big mouth. Bear hollering and biting and snapping, slapping hisself upside his own jaws, steady smashing bees, but the Kamikazes don't give a fuck. They dives straight down, deep down inside Brer Bear's soft, pink parts—sting his throat and stomach and liver and lungs. Insides stinging like fire drive that big ole bear crazy with pain. Bear start to roll round on the ground, choking, throwing up whole weeks of dinner, spitting big globs of bee and honey till he wobble back up on all fours and hauls ass, gone like a turkey through the corn. Wish he ain't never heard of bees nor honey. Wish he ain't never been born. Ain't much beehive left behind. But you know how busy bees is. In no time they got that hive up and buzzing again.

Strange thing is, all them chewed-up gobs of bee and honey and food and blood the bear throwed up. Not all the Kamikaze bees dead in there. A few crawls out the mess. Maybe they a little sticky and beat to shit, but a couple few alive. Alive and just as wild, mean and crazy as ever. Brer Bear come back, they gone bust his big chops wide open again.

Damn. You snoring already, Till. Bet you smiling over there. Knew you'd like them Kamikaze bees, Till.